In Search of
Ancient
North America

In Search of
Ancient
North America

An Archaeological Journey
to Forgotten Cultures

Heather Pringle

John Wiley & Sons, Inc.

New York • Chichester • Brisbane • Toronto • Singapore

Copyright © 1996 by Heather Pringle
Published by John Wiley & Sons, Inc.

Library of Congress Cataloging-in-Publication Data:
Pringle, Heather Anne
    In search of ancient North America : an archaeological journey to forgotten cultures / Heather Pringle.
      p.   cm.
    Includes bibliographical references.
    ISBN 0-471-04237-4 (cloth : alk. paper)
    1. Indians of North America—Antiquities. 2. Excavations (Archaeology)—North America. 3. North America—Antiquities. I. Title.
E77.9.P58   1996
970.01—dc20   95-43781

Printed in the United States of America
10 9 8 7 6 5 4 3 2 1

For Geoff.
And for Gretta, whose love
of words remains with me still.

Acknowledgments

Writing a book about archaeology, like excavating a site, is something of a tribal affair. Certainly, this book would never have seen the light of day without the kind deeds and assistance of many people. First, I'd like to thank the researchers who welcomed me with such hospitality to their sites, taught me something of flint-knapping and bannock-making, and later read through my prose with expert eyes: Jacques Cinq-Mars, Mark Raab, Andy Yatsko, Solveig Turpin, Brian Hayden, Mark Lynott, Brad Lepper, Tom Windes, Bruce Bradley, Tim Pauketat, Melvin Fowler, Jack Brink, Brian Reeves, Dean Knight, and Gary Warrick. Thanks, too, go to their varied crews, whose good humor and entertaining stories of surfing, sharks, and snakes made time fly in the field.

I am also extremely grateful to The Canada Council, whose generous financial assistance permitted me to complete my research. Without its help, this book could never have been finished. Thanks, too, go to *Equinox* magazine, for originally assigning me the stories that became the seeds of this book, and to the Canadian Museum of Civilization, the Polar Continental Shelf Project, the U.S. Navy, The Rock Art Foundation, and the United States National Park Service for providing invaluable logistical support—from helicopter flights to much appreciated accommodations.

My heartfelt thanks also go to Sandy Taylor, whose sound advice has contributed much to this book, and to my editor, Emily Loose, for her astute comments on the manuscript. I'd also like to express my appreciation to Carolyn Boyd, N'omi Greber, Anna Sofaer, and David Wilcox, who took time out from busy research schedules to read parts of the manuscript. This book has benefited greatly from all these eyes. The responsibility for errors and omissions, however, rests firmly with the author.

Last but definitely not least, I'd like to thank John Masters, Andrew Nikiforuk, Alex L. Pringle, Alex D. Pringle, and Sheila Greckol for their lavish encouragement and moral support. And my deepest gratitude goes to my husband, Geoff Lakeman, whose humor and wit remain a constant source of joy, lightening even the labor pains of writing.

Heather Pringle

Contents

Contents

Conclusion

Further Readings

Bibliography

Index

1. Bluefish Caves; 2. Eel Point; 3. The Lower Pecos; 4. Keatley Creek; 5. Hopeton Earthworks; 6. Chaco Canyon; 7. Cahokia; 8. Head-Smashed-In Buffalo Jump; 9. Ball site.

Introduction

O n an early spring day in 1975, a solemn party of native elders swept down the echoing hallways of the Provincial Museum of Alberta in Canada, where I worked as a young research assistant. Wrapped in woolen blankets, they spoke softly in their native Blackfoot, then turned and disappeared into a curatorial office. I had seen the slender man accompanying them weeks before. Indeed, Adolf Hungry Wolf had become a frequent figure in the museum as he gathered materials for a tribal history. But that afternoon, Hungry Wolf had little interest in sorting through photos or dog-eared documents. Unknown to any but his companions, he had awakened the previous winter from a troubling dream: In it, he and tribal elders had spirited away an ancient and sacred Blackfoot shrine from museum exhibits.

During the 1960s, a destitute ceremonialist of the Blood tribe in southern Alberta had sold the Longtime Medicine Pipe Bundle for $3,000. Bringing it to Edmonton, curatorial staff members had untied its wrappings, laying out vermilion-streaked animal skins, pouches of paint, and a beautiful stone pipe in glass display cases. On the Blood reserve, word of the sale spread. Influential elders met quietly with officials, entreating them to return the ancient shrine. But museum administrators demurred, unwilling to part with such a rare and valuable find. On that distant spring morning in 1975, Hungry Wolf and his three companions had arrived at the museum determined to carry out the dream's bidding.

With grave faces, they asked to bear the bundle outdoors for prayer, as was the tradition. Seeing no simple way of refusing, embarrassed officials began rounding up the pieces. The elders waited patiently in a large back room. When all was ready at last, the small party formed a procession, heading down the hallway and out the doors, past surveillance cameras and watchful guards, security systems and curious onlookers. Museum staff trailed at a discreet distance. Circling the building and praying with the bundle in hand, the elders rounded the corner of the parking lot. Suddenly, without warning, the leader, a stoop-shouldered man named Many Gray Horses, broke into a sprint. From behind, someone shouted. Seeing a prized exhibit disappear before his eyes, the museum director charged. But at the final moment, he drew up short. With immense dignity, the elders climbed into a dusty truck. Then, just as Hungry Wolf had dreamed, they wheeled out into traffic, setting off for home with the bundle.

On the Blood Reserve, grizzled elders still talk about the day many years ago when Hungry Wolf and Many Gray Horses cast a charm over the museum. And I think they are right. Certainly what happened on that spring afternoon more than twenty years ago made an indelible impression on me. Although I had grown up just a few hundred miles north of the Blood Indian Reserve, I knew almost nothing about the native past of this land. As a student of history, I had learned little of the traditional culture that honored such bundles; I had no idea when the Blood had first wandered these northern grasslands or how they had earned a living from a land some early European scientists wrote off as virtually uninhabitable. But I sensed that something tantalizing and profound lay in these matters: Many Gray Horses and Hungry Wolf had convinced me of that.

That glimpse of traditional Blackfoot culture launched a long and fascinating quest, one that I pursued as a journalist during the 1980s and 1990s. Deeply impressed, I scoured historic records and met Blackfoot ceremonialists, who permitted me to watch as they unwrapped their sacred bundles for the health and prosperity of their people. I peered into musty collections of small museums and talked with archaeologists such as Brian Reeves who took me out along prairie fields studded with centuries-old tepee rings. An expert on the prehistory of the northern plains, Reeves explained that the Blackfoot bundles dated back centuries. In a New York museum, he had examined one Buffalo Catchers Society Bundle at least 330 years old: Each spring, upon opening the bundle, the owner had carved a new notch in the fire stick. And it preserved ancient memory. Along the stem of the sacred pipe hung a small lock of horsehair. So sacred was this bundle to the Blackfoot, explained Reeves, that the hair likely came from the first horse ever seen by the plains hunters in the early eighteenth century. (Such a horse would have descended from herds first introduced to North America by Spanish soldiers. The continent's native horses, five species in all, perished at the end of the last Ice Age.)

Intrigued, I found myself pulling out tattered maps of North America, pressing flat the frayed folds. I was consumed with curiosity. What other long-vanished peoples shaped their lives to wave-washed coasts and rainless deserts? What mysterious peoples once ranged the cool northern forests and torpid southern bayous? North America, after all, is the world's third largest landmass. It spans nearly 9 million square miles from the frozen fringes of the Canadian Arctic to the steamy coasts of Panama, from a few degrees short of the North Pole to a few degrees shy of the equator. It is an immense, almost unimaginable, sprawl of land, one equaling in latitudinal range the vast territories that spread from northern Siberia to India. In such expanses in the Old World, hundreds of strange and exotic cultures, from Siberian mammoth hunters to Scythian horsemen, flourished and foundered over thousands of years of prehistory. Had North America witnessed something comparable?

The answers lay buried in scientific literature. To unearth small fragments of the continent's mysterious past, antiquarians and scientists began mounting excavations as early as the eighteenth century and later invented a new word—*prehistory*—to describe a past before written language. One of the earliest of all scientific investigators on the continent was a man with an insatiable sense of curiosity, Thomas Jefferson. At a time when American intellectuals gave scarcely a thought to the continent's shrouded prehistory, Jefferson relished such matters. Listening to the tales of friend William Bartram, a naturalist who had roamed the American Southeast at a time when Choctaw families still buried their dead in earthen mounds, the future American president pondered whether earthworks near his Virginia home had served a similar purpose. In what was likely the first scientific excavation on the continent, he cut a great trench through a mound along the Rivanna River—"that I might examine its internal structure" (Silverberg 1968). The human bones embedded in the upper layers, he noted, were better preserved than those at the bottom. None bore battle wounds, as one might expect in a mass grave. In all likelihood, Jefferson concluded, native mourners had interred their dead there over a considerable period of time.

The Rivanna excavation was a remarkable piece of early work, but few contemporary scholars shared Jefferson's enthusiasm. Indeed, most who followed in the nineteenth century eschewed careful science, devoting themselves instead to collecting antiquities for private and public collections. Hiring day laborers or enlisting the help of a curious public, these field-workers tunneled through villages and hunting camps, blundering blindly as they searched for fine pottery and basketry, carved stone figurines, and effigy pipes. Few saw any reason to jot down their observations as they worked. (Indeed, after excavating nearly 200 rooms in the greathouse of Pueblo Bonito in Chaco Canyon—one of the most important ruins on the continent—one early-twentieth-century researcher could produce little more than two shoe boxes stuffed with filing cards to show for his efforts.)

While such expeditions produced some of the continent's finest museum collections, the hunt for antiquities and the ransacking of ruins literally destroyed major sites. And under pressure from their museum employers, many early researchers began zeroing in on prehistoric cemeteries and mortuary facilities, where treasures such as jade adzes, turquoise beads, copper headdresses—sure to appeal to museum audiences—sometimes lined graves of the dead. Such excavations had a disastrous effect. As the work proceeded, many native leaders came to see archaeologists and their field crews as little better than grave robbers—a bitter legacy that lingers in Canada and the United States to this day.

The rabid quest for artifacts and the excavation of tombs, moreover, yielded scant information about the *lives* of those who roamed the continent in times past. But North American researchers were slow to see this as a problem. Like many other members of nineteenth-century society, they saw native tribes as primitive and naive, childlike wastrels who had long preferred the adrenaline of the hunt to the drudgery of building civilizations. Native people, concluded Ohio scholar Caleb Atwater in 1820, were "men in a savage state, little versed in the arts of civilized life" (Silverberg, 1968). And such attitudes stifled curiosity. If these were simple savages, after all, they had likely seen few changes since the time of biblical creation.

Throughout the nineteenth century, this racism actively shaped archaeological thought. When the great English naturalist Charles Darwin published his theories on evolution in 1859, suggesting that natural selection of the fittest had produced ever more complex forms of life, prehistorians quickly pricked up their ears. If human beings had evolved from less intelligent primates, perhaps human cultures, too, had clambered up a grand ladder of progress. Before long, English scholar Sir John Lubbock published a highly influential book, *Pre-historic Times, as Illustrated by Ancient Remains, and the Manners and Customs of Modern Savages,* concluding that European culture represented the pinnacle of human cultural evolution; tribal groups in North America, on the other hand, occupied the lowest rungs.

For a while, these theories of cultural evolution enjoyed considerable vogue among American and English intellectuals. But as the new century dawned, a certain skepticism set in. Like other scholars of the time, archaeologists began questioning the benefits of technological progress. Before long, they quietly jettisoned notions of cultural ladders. But even so, few seriously believed that North American tribal cultures were ancient. In the absence of much evidence, most suggested that Asian migrants had colonized the continent relatively recently—within the past 4,000 years or so. And if North America had been peopled so late, went the logic, it could never have boasted a wealth of prehistoric cultures.

Archaeologists had clearly reached a brick wall, one not easily scaled. But it was just then, in the opening years of the twentieth century, that new advances in excavation helped unlock the door to the continent's shadowy past. Observant researchers noted that certain forces such as strong winds, floods, and melting snow deposited telltale sediments on the earth, creating distinctive layers over time. In undisturbed sites, the youngest strata lay on top; the oldest at the bottom. These seemingly simple observations proved invaluable for archaeology. By peeling off layers along a prehistoric house floor or refuse heap and studying the stone tools, pottery fragments, and other debris embedded within, archaeologists could discern major changes in human activities over time.

Intrigued, a handful of North American researchers began applying stratigraphic methods to their digs. In the American Southwest, Alfred Kidder launched what was then the largest excavation in North America, gently stripping off the minute layers. The results proved intriguing. Contrary to earlier belief, Kidder and his colleagues detected striking changes in pottery styles over time, piecing together clear evidence of a succession of cultures. Other North American archaeologists soon followed Kidder's example. Before long, crews began toppling conventional views of North American prehistory. While excavating an Ice Age fossil bed in New Mexico in 1927, for example, a crew from the Colorado Museum of Natural History unearthed a stone spearpoint lying next to the rib of a long-extinct species of bison. The find was the first solid proof that humans had ranged this continent for at least 10,000 years. With just one dig, team members had more than doubled the time span of North American prehistory.

As the din surrounding the discovery subsided, archaeologists took stock. Impressed by the new time depth of human life on the continent and armed now with revealing methods of excavation, they began scouring North America for ancient, densely layered campsites and villages. Now seeking signs of cultural change, they found them everywhere, in the Mississippi River valley, the Great Basin, the high Arctic. And as the Second World War ended, the science of physics provided researchers with a new way of dating sites. In the late 1940s, Willard Libby, a future Nobel Laureate, discovered that all living creatures ingest minute quantities of radiocarbon from the atmosphere. When an animal or plant dies, its radiocarbon decays at a predictable rate. By measuring traces of radiation from prehistoric bones in a site, scientists could determine when the animals had perished and hence when hunters had consumed them there.

Today, archaeology is a hard science, one that borrows liberally from other disciplines. Amassing data on soil types, fossil pollen, geological formations, regional climatic patterns, and ancient faunal species at sites, archaeologists struggle to reconstruct long-vanished environments. Mapping three-dimensional positions of artifacts and features; classifying finds such as projectile points and pottery shards; dating diverse layers by methods as varied as radiocarbon, archaeomagnetic, tree-ring, thermoluminescence, and obsidian hydration tests; and sifting through analysts' reports on such arcane subjects as DNA analyses of ancient hair samples or microscopic wear patterns on tools, archaeologists take enormous pains to wrest every possible scrap of information from research sites.

In the end, surrounded by a bewildering welter of data, they search for patterns—chronological and spatial—and clues to their interpretations. The disappearance of butchered sea-lion bones over time in the deposits of an ancient coastal camp may hint, for example, that ballooning populations of sea hunters wiped out the vulnerable mammals. The sudden appearance of a strange new type of ceremonial pottery in desert pueblos some 600 years ago may reveal the appearance of a powerful new religious cult. While archaeologists must muster much evidence to prove such fledgling theories, these obscure patterns and trends are the building blocks of North American prehistory. And it is by fitting them together that we are now able to envision the rise and fall of ancient cultures, to glimpse the lives of artists and shamans, farmers and lords, whose voices, as Linnaeus once noted, "are now only able to whisper, when everything else has become silent."

Through the scientific literature, I have begun to see a continent peopled with rich and now vanished cultures—the whale-hunting Thule people of the Canadian Arctic who elevated gadgetry to high art; the salmon-fishing cultures of the interior plateau whose people wore salmon-skin shoes and counted their wealth in salmon oil; the desert-loving Mimbres who pierced their funerary bowls with holes to allow the spirits within to join those of the dead; the plains bison hunters who once snared the blessings of the sun in great medicine wheels. Through archaeology, through the ingenious methods of hundreds of researchers working in digs and laboratories across Canada and the United States, we can now see what had been previously hidden from sight—the breathtaking prehistory of our continent.

And what I find most staggering now is the sheer antiquity, diversity, and complexity of ancient life in North America. Although many conservative archaeologists still stick to the view that Asian migrants landed here at the very end of the last Ice Age some 12,000 years ago, a new and ever growing body of research suggests that they first journeyed to the New World much, much earlier. Indeed, many liberal researchers now place the arrival of humans between 21,000 and 42,000 years ago—at the height of the last Ice Age. Leaving behind Eurasia, a great rolling grassland where modern humans and quite possibly Neanderthal hunters still stalked mammoths, these small bands of hunters settled in a vast, new, mysterious continent.

Just who these first North Americans were and what kind of culture they possessed remain the subject of intense scientific inquiry. We do know, however, that they mastered one of the harshest environments on earth, thanks to a remarkable knowledge of Arctic clothing, shelter, and animal behavior. And over time, their adventuresome descendents spread throughout the length and breadth of the continent. As François Bordes, a famous French Paleolithic scholar, once observed, this march southward was the longest expanse ever colonized by humans, an accomplishment not to be equaled again "until man lands on a planet belonging to another star" (Bordes 1968).

Fanning out in North America, these early bands settled regions as remote as the Aucilla River in Florida, Murray Springs in Arizona, and the Debert site in Nova Scotia. And 11,000 years ago, when the Ice Age game they depended upon began vanishing from the continent—whether from overhunting, as some scholars suggest, or from the disappearance of the sprawling grasslands—they proved eminently flexible. Adapting over the millennia to regions as varied as coastal plains, deserts, and subtropical swamps, they devised hundreds of ingenious new ways of earning a living. In the searing heat of southern Texas, they gathered the starchy roots of desert succulents and killed fish with potent poisons. In the rain forests of the Queen Charlotte Islands, they wove hats and capes of cedar bark and built sprawling cedar-plank houses. In the northern Arctic, they harpooned whales from immense sealskin boats.

By the second millennium B.C., families in eastern North America had invented agriculture. No longer bound to hunt daily, they soon found time for increasingly elaborate forms of art, astronomy, architecture, and religious ceremony. In the Southeast and the Southwest, ample food supplies gave rise to ever more complex forms of social organization—complete with powerful priests and illustrious lords—by the beginning of the tenth century A.D. Indeed, two very different but immensely powerful regional capitals suddenly blazed north of the Rio Grande: Chaco Canyon in present-day New Mexico and Cahokia along the floodplain of the Mississippi River. So complex were their economies, politics, sciences, and ceremonial practices that archaeologists are only now beginning to appreciate the full richness of these societies.

Fascinated by this growing body of research, I have long wanted to journey to North America's premiere prehistoric sites, accompanying leading archaeologists and their crews into the field. In the early 1990s, I started drawing up plans. Sitting down with thick stacks of scientific papers and books, I began compiling a short list of sites. I wanted to span the millennia—from the days when Siberian mammoth hunters first pitched camp in North America to the time when Europeans landed on these shores—and to cover as much ground in Canada and the United States as I possibly could. (I put aside Mexico and Central America in favor of concentrating on lesser-known prehistoric terrain.) I also wanted to find sites that shed critical new light on some of the key themes in North American archaeology—the origins of religion, the rise of inequality and complex social hierarchies, the emergence of agriculture, and the extent of prehistoric trade.

In the end, I picked out nine major study areas, from the untrammeled forests of the Yukon to the cactus-covered valleys of Texas. At Bluefish Caves, a small team struggled to recover traces of the earliest North Americans. On the remote island of San Clemente, a crew of surfer-archaeologists puzzled over the ways in which early humans plundered the marine world. In the Lower Pecos, gun-toting Texans deciphered the origins of art in North America. In a sagebrush-covered canyon in British Columbia, an irreverent west coast archaeologist unraveled the rise of private property. In southern Ohio, researchers raced to uncover vestiges of early agriculture. In New Mexico, an archaeoastronomer puzzled over the roads emanating from a mysterious prehistoric capital. Near the city of St. Louis, a brilliant young Mississippian scholar unearthed the remarkable tale of a divine lord. Near the steep fringe of the Rockies in southern Alberta, researchers exhumed the debris of a vast continental trade. And in the Great Lakes region, an ingenious Ontario archaeologist tracked down the carriers of devastating Old World epidemics.

Over the course of ten months, I traveled to eight of these sites. (I had earlier written an extensive magazine story on one of my selections, Head-Smashed-In Buffalo Jump; I subsequently expanded the article to accommodate new research.) Journeying by helicopter and rickety DC-3, riverboat and rust-bitten Volvo, I camped out with field crews and headed off to work with them each morning. In Chaco Canyon, they drilled tree-ring cores from the beams and rafters of greathouses; on San Clemente Island, they hefted 55-pound buckets of shattered abalone shell from the pits, screening them in search of tiny fish bones; at Cahokia, they spent hours hunched over plastic basins, cleaning and washing clay-caked pottery shards. Working shoulder to shoulder with them, I gained a new and deep appreciation of their meticulous labor. Underlying the elegant theory and the ingenious detective work are hours of trying toil in the field and in the lab.

The appeal of this work varies enormously from researcher to researcher. For some, archaeology amounts to a great intellectual challenge, elusive, tantalizing, always engaging, always worth the chase. For others, it is more a grand adventure, the stuff of legends, pursued in unbridled freedom in remote and often breathtaking wilderness. But what joins all of these archaeologists finally, I think, is the deep desire to span the gulf of time, connecting in some intimate way with those who are now little more than rags and bones. Unarticulated, often unacknowledged, this desire is a profound longing for communion with those who walked here before.

The chapters that follow chronicle these strange and wonderful journeys into the field and the people I met there. It is about archaeology as it is practiced today and what this little-understood science now tells us about the obscure prehistory of a continent. It is about thunder lords and sacred roads, buffalo stones and turquoise graves. It is about the continual frustration of trying to wrest knowledge from the slenderest of clues and the astonishing amount of information that can be wrung from bones and stones and shards.

Last, but not least, this book is about a kind of wonder that grips the imagination of those who unravel the past. A few years ago, I talked to an archaeologist who had recently led excavations in Chaco Canyon in New Mexico. Each morning, she told me, she rose at dawn and set out immediately for the greathouse of Chetro Ketl, arriving well before her crew. Working in solitude there, she often glanced up at the fingerprints and handprints left 900 years earlier by those who had plastered the wall. And many mornings she would find herself reaching up and fitting her own hand in these prints. "You can't really get past that," she told me, shaking her head, a little embarrassed. "But that's why I went into archaeology."

1

DARK PASSAGES

Bluefish Caves, Yukon Territory

Let us probe the silent places,
Let us see what luck betide us.

—ROBERT SERVICE

For much of his career, three decades of lonely, trouble-some, some might say thankless, work, Jacques Cinq-Mars has wandered imagined worlds. On this clear summer afternoon, one of the warmest of the year, the grizzled archaeologist stubs out his cigarette and stares up at the dark slit in the rock high above. His face creased as a crumpled bag, eyes curious and alert, he folds a large map dotted with dozens of cryptic notes and tucks it into his pack. Then he gazes back up to the black cavern. A look somewhere between weariness and hopeless longing crosses his face. "You feel there might be something there," he says finally, a faint smile toying at his mouth.

Gruff and irascible, little given to fancies or nonsense, Cinq-Mars has come to the northern Yukon on an elusive quest—to track down slender vestiges of early Siberian wanderers in the New World. It's not work for the faint of heart. Sprawling for thousands of square miles above the Arctic Circle, encompassing an area larger than all Scotland, the northern Yukon is a vast wilderness of boreal forest and barren rock. Seamed by rivers and streams, edged by rampartlike mountains, it remains much as it has for centuries, home to caribou, moose, grizzly, and hunters from the Gwich'in tribe. Cinq-Mars, however, refuses to quit. A veteran archaeologist, he knows something's out there.

Tugging down a battered canvas fishing hat, he glances over at assistant Stringer Charlie, a quiet man in a blue-flowered shirt, baseball cap, and jeans. Reaching for a dusty cannister of carbide, Charlie begins the slow trek up the slope, some sixty-five miles southeast of the tiny Yukon village of Old Crow. Cinq-Mars and I follow. Along the far wall of the canyon, snow glitters in high, thin patches, a perpetual reminder of the winter to come. On this sunny, southern slope, however, summer prevails briefly. Hauling himself up, panting a little with the effort, Cinq-Mars climbs in silence. And as he reaches the dark cave mouth, he is all attention. Along the ground, he spies a small black ball of leather. He picks it up and passes it on, all scholarly interest. It is the paw of a porcupine recently consumed by a grizzly.

Cinq-Mars shrugs and presses into the cave, eager to explore its gloomy unknown. Standing there, I wonder, not for the first time, if he really knows what he's doing. But I can see no graceful way out. Sliding on a helmet and carbide headlamp, I turn into the cold dark tunnel. In the chamber ahead, Cinq-Mars is less than pleased. Rocks rolling down the steep entranceway have swept away whatever trace of ancient hearths may once have lingered here; the walls reveal no sign of fires, no smear of red paint. "I'm sure that at one time or another someone passed through and poked around," says Cinq-Mars finally, his French-Canadian accent soft as down. "But it's not the location that I'm looking for."

Restless, argumentative, forever dissatisfied, Cinq-Mars is still chasing after clues to the Ice Age mysteries at Bluefish Caves, forty miles southwest of Old Crow. Little known outside a small circle of experts, never yet fully published, Bluefish Caves remain nothing more than a tantalizing name to most archaeologists. And yet, within these three small caverns, Cinq-Mars, a curator at the Canadian Museum of Civilization in Hull, Quebec, has amassed the most convincing and detailed evidence yet that Asian tribes flourished in North America more than 23,000 years ago—11,000 years earlier than many researchers currently credit. "I'm now in a position to state that Bluefish Caves represent the oldest known archaeological site in the North America," he observes solemnly, "and one of the oldest in the world."

Such claims are neither rashly made nor swiftly accepted. While experts have long agreed that the first colonists were Siberian hunters who journeyed over what is now the Bering Strait to northern Alaska and the northern Yukon, they are now battling bitterly over the timing. On one side stand conservatives who argue, based on a cautious reading of the published archaeological record, that Asian migrants first stepped foot in the New World some 12,000 years ago and spread as far as the South American pampas in just a millenium. On the other gather more liberal researchers who theorize that the Siberians landed here much earlier—a position increasingly supported by linguistic studies of modern native peoples and genetic analyses of human DNA—and migrated much more slowly south. Perfectly honed to the rigors of Arctic life, they suggest, these northern Asians would have required thousands of years to adapt to the diseases, climates, and prey of southern ecological zones.

The sticking point has always been hard archaeological proof. But Cinq-Mars believes he has finally unearthed the critical shreds of evidence in Bluefish Caves. If he is right, the three small Yukon caves will one day rewrite the opening chapters of North American prehistory and reshape expert thinking on subjects as diverse as ancient trade and Ice Age ecology. Authorities have suggested, for example, that this far northern corner of the continent was a blustery polar desert during the peak of the last glaciation, some 30,000 to 18,000 years ago. But bone beds at Bluefish Caves reveal a radically different picture—a northern steppe replete with herds of horses and steppe bison and prides of lions. How did early humans fare here? And who were these people? Bone tools from the lowlands near Bluefish Caves now suggest that hunters stalked the

Yukon as early as 40,000 years ago—at a time when both modern humans and their nearest kin, the Neanderthals, roamed the Old World. To some researchers, these findings raise a tantalizing question: Who arrived first in the New World?

But as he tromps through the tiny Gwich'in settlement of Old Crow this June morning, trudging past the nursing station and school, smokehouses and satellite dishes, Cinq-Mars clearly has other matters on his mind. Stowing tripod and pack outside the settlement's small airport, he ducks into the office to thank weather observer Helen Keedwell for a recent loan of ground caribou meat. Coffee in hand, he gazes out at the loading area, where a lanky mechanic fuels up our helicopter—the only aircraft in sight. At nine o'clock in the morning, the sky is bright blue, the temperature in the high sixties. But already black insects dance frantically against the glass. Cinq-Mars shakes his head. "The mosquitoes will be bad today," he says gruffly, reaching into a pocket for his tobacco.

Rumpled and unshaven, with gold-rimmed glasses, bushy mustache, and long, dark hair combed straight back, the fifty-four-year-old scientist looks every bit the old Yukon hand, a character straight from the pages of poet Robert Service. Dressed, as he generally is during field season, in shapeless brown pants, plaid shirt, and canvas fishing vest, he seems as much a part of this small northern settlement as the weather-worn cabins and the rolling river beyond. Conversant with everything from local genealogy to co-op politics, he knows just about everyone in this village of some 250, and everyone, from children to stooped elders, seem to know him. And yet for all his love of the north, all his stoic acceptance of icy tents, thin bedrolls, and tormenting insects, Cinq-Mars belongs to a very different life.

Born just outside Montreal in Longueuil, the rugged archaeologist was raised in the lap of privilege. The son of a successful architect, the grandson of a distinguished translator, poet, and sculptor, he thrived in a wealthy French-Canadian family fond of art, culture, and debate. Educated by the Jesuits, the young scholar soon enrolled as an undergraduate at the University of Montreal, discovering an unforeseen aptitude for anthropology. Spending a year in France, at the Institute of Prehistory in Bordeaux headed by the preeminent French archaeologist François Bordes, he immersed himself in studies of hunting-and-gathering peoples in Paleolithic or Stone Age Europe, developing a lifelong fascination for the subject.

But already the adventuresome student had acquired a taste for the raw beauty of the Yukon. Signing on to a field crew led by Canadian archaeologist William Irving in 1966, Cinq-Mars had begun spending summers in the Old Crow region, assisting on digs. Linked to southern Canada only by barge and the occasional bush plane, Old Crow was still firmly entrenched in the past. Cinq-Mars quickly fell under its charms. On Saturday nights, he and other crew members would drift downriver to dances in the community hall. "I close my eyes and I can can still see it," he says. Women dressed in their finest shawls and slippers lined one end of the room; men the other. Children pressed their faces against the windows. And as the local fiddlers warmed up the floor, the formality melted like butter. The widows were the wildest. "We'd get *grabbed* for a dance," he recalls.

And the fieldwork was proving strangely seductive, too, as Irving and others scrambled to make sense of the Ice Age past. Studies had shown that a series of global deep freezes, beginning some 2.5 million years ago and ending 10,000 years before the present, had periodically lowered the world's sea levels, baring a broad land bridge from Siberia to Alaska. Far more than a slender isthmus, this expansive landmass, a kind of northern Atlantis, had strangely altered arctic weather patterns, creating an arid polar climate. Free of heavy winter snowfall, lands from the Verkhoyansk Mountains in Siberia to the Mackenzie River in Canada had largely escaped advancing ice. While much of Canada and the northern United States groaned beneath steep walls of snow and ice, Beringia, as this vast northland came to be known, remained a green, grassy outpost, beckoning to wildlife. "So the whole notion of refugia came along," says Cinq-Mars.

Researchers interested in the peopling of the New World pricked up their ears. If southern animals had fled to Beringia, why not tribes of early humans? "There was a lot of thinking about these issues," says Cinq-Mars. The northern Yukon promised to be a hot spot. While gathering the bones of mammoths and steppe bison from major Ice Age fossil beds along the Old Crow River, Canadian zoologist Richard Harington and his assistant happened upon something startling—a caribou bone whose end had been shaped into a row of small teeth. Made for stripping flesh from skins, the mysterious tool had the same reddish stain as the Ice Age bones. Fascinated, Irving shifted his field operations north, setting Cinq-Mars and others to work prying thousands of fossils from the frozen banks of the Old Crow River.

It was grueling work, with few obvious rewards. Team members never collected another tool quite like the caribou-bone flesher. But Irving was fired with a kind of faith. Picking through the fossil carnage carefully, he began poring over strange spiral fractures and flaking patterns that distinguished many of the mammoth remains. Nature, he concluded, had not shattered bones this way; humans had. And he soon mustered impressive support for his contention. Detailed studies by American flint-knapping expert Robson Bonnichsen showed that the heavy mammoth bones had been worked while fresh by chipping and flaking techniques similar to those used on stone tools by Paleolithic hunters in the Old World. Moreover, the samples appeared ancient. American radiocarbon experts dated two worked mammoth bones and the original flesher to 27,000 years ago—the oldest known relics of human life, it seemed, in the New World.

The resulting paper in *Science* set off a wave of fierce controversy. Far from being human handiwork, noted critics, the mammoth bones had been shattered by river ice, trampled by large animals, or gnawed by hungry carnivores. Other experts raised troubling doubts about the precise procedures employed by the radiocarbon laboratory. Undaunted, Irving and his team pressed on with the research. All the bone tools gathered from the Old Crow banks had been swept there by the river from some distant location and redeposited in a hopeless jumble. What Irving craved now more than anything was an undisturbed site.

While colleague Richard Morlan began combing the valley bottoms of the Old Crow and Bell Rivers, Irving, along with Cinq-Mars, who was working on his doctoral degree, scouted the remote uplands by helicopter. But nothing went as hoped. Searching vast tracts of dense boreal forest without detailed maps or any real inkling of where Ice Age tribes had camped or hunted was akin to scouring the universe for intelligent life; the odds were stacked steeply against them. "Visibility is zilch in terms of archaeology," says Cinq-Mars today, shaking his head. "You really have to look for things before you can find them."

Still, no one was ready to pack it in. And in the late summer of 1975, while skimming over the rolling foothills of the Keele Range by helicopter, Cinq-Mars and others in the crew noticed a small cave overlooking the Bluefish River, named for the aqua-colored arctic grayling that swam in its waters. Curious, they landed. While the caves resembled little more than carnivore dens, they could conceal scraps of Beringian fauna—something that might help reconstruct the ancient environment. Jotting down a few notes, Cinq-Mars decided to return. This was his first glimpse of Bluefish Caves.

✦   ✦   ✦

As the helicopter beats its way south this morning, Cinq-Mars peers out the side window, silently tracing the coffee-colored course of the Bluefish River. In the early morning air, a warm wind laps against the craft, rocking it gently like a cradle. In the back, I sit in silence, absorbed by the view. Enveloped by clear, blue sky, I can see all the way west into the deep green valleys of Alaska, all the way south to the tundra-covered peaks of the Keele Range. Below stretches mile upon mile of dark forest and looping river. Gazing down from this godly height, I sway uncertainly between guilt and fascination—guilt at invading this wild green world by machine, fascination at the seemingly infinite variations on the theme of water and tree.

Ahead, in the distance, Cinq-Mars points out a slender border of gray atop a high forested hill. Dwarfed by its surroundings, the stony ridge of Bluefish Caves seems scarcely to warrant a second look, more a thinning of spruce than any definable shape. But as we pull closer and pilot Woody McBride banks steeply, I can see gray fingerlike spurs and, finally, along the southern edges, small dark gashes in the rock. Perched along the high rim of this immense primordial valley, Bluefish Caves look tiny, fragile, and slight, like some hapless outpost set down on a distant planet.

Shouldering our packs and setting off through swarms of mosquitoes half an hour later, Cinq-Mars and I follow a well-worn path along the ridge to the shadowy recesses of Cave 1. Weathered and rough-hewn, carpeted in rubble, the rugged cavern stretches just 13 feet into the cliffside—the slenderest and least hospitable of shelters. Yet it was here that team members first came across traces of Beringian hunters. While cleaning the bottom of a test pit in 1978, Raymond LeBlanc unearthed an intriguing fragment of flintlike chert. On closer look, it proved to be a microblade, a type of tiny sharp-edged tool first fashioned in the Old World and found in some of the oldest Alaskan sites. "We all joked about the fact that he had planted it," says Cinq-Mars, "and I gave him shit, making silly jokes like that." But a few days later, while troweling through another square, Cinq-Mars picked out a second microblade, this time at a level that had yielded remains of an extinct Ice Age horse the previous year.

Elated, he expanded excavations. And as crew members bent to their work, gleaning a few more tool fragments, they puzzled over scattered pockets of animal bone. While some resembled the droppings or pellets of predators, others revealed clear signs of human activity. Just beyond the cave mouth, for example, Cinq-Mars and his team struck a bony pavement that sprawled for nearly six yards across the slope. Strewn with skeletal remains of horses and other large mammals, the fractured heap looked suspiciously like butchering refuse. Indeed, some of the bones bore clear knife marks.

An aerial view of the stony ridge containing Bluefish Caves. The Bluefish River meanders below. (Courtesy of the author.)

Close-up of the entrance to one of the two principal caves. (Courtesy of Jacques Cinq-Mars.)

Kneeling beside these heaps, lifting shattered skull and pelvis from the cool soil, Cinq-Mars wondered if ancient butchers here had carved up their prey exactly where they fell. Most of the bones belonged to herd animals; a natural trap lay close at hand. Stepping back from the mouth of the cave, Cinq-Mars points to the ridgetop. "There's a very nice slope behind, moving up towards the cliff," he observes. "It's a blind break that you have there." If hunters had combined their forces to stampede a small herd over this cliff, others hovering below could make short work of the wounded.

Historically, Gwich'in in the region had profited from similar collective acts. In countryside to the north, they had stampeded caribou into drive lanes enclosed by hand-built wooden fences. And evidence clearly suggests that some Old World hunters had perfected herd hunting, too. Beneath the cliffs of Solutré in France, for example, researchers discovered the bones of thousands of Ice Age horses dating back 17,000 years. So it is quite possible, says Cinq-Mars, that Eurasian migrants brought these methods with them to the

Trench with skull and pelvis bones of herd animals. (Courtesy of Jacques Cinq-Mars.)

New World. "My feeling, and it's only that, is that it wasn't invented here. It was what allowed people to live in arctic and subarctic environments."

But while the excavations were fascinating, not all was smooth sailing. Setting aside part of the cave floor for future research—a practice favored by responsible excavators—Cinq-Mars returned in 1981 to an archaeologist's worst nightmare: The neat individual layers had mysteriously dissolved into a homogenous silty jelly. "When you open up a site like this," he says, a note of frustration edging his voice, "you completely change the thermal environment. In wintertime and especially in springtime, the frozen ground will do horrible things to the sediment." The rest of the cave, and all its secrets, lay mired in mud.

With a shrug, Cinq-Mar turns and leads the way around the corner. Brushing a swarm of mosquitoes from his shoulder, he stops in front of a small hollow on the other side of the spur. Known today as Cave 2, the small cavern opens out on a sweeping view of the river valley. To Cinq-Mars, it has always looked like a superb roost for human hunters, and in the early 1980s, he and his crew set to work here. Before long their spirits began to lift. Along the lower sediments, team members collected more fragments of worked chert—microblades; cores from which microblades had been struck; short, pointed blade tools known as *burins*, ideal for shaving bone, ivory, and antler; and tiny chips splintered from burin edges. Cinq-Mars was entranced. Carefully refitting the tiny chips back on some of the burins, he could see that the Bluefish hunters had sharpened their carving tools right in the cave. "This implies that they did work bone or antler or ivory here."

And these hunters had gone to considerable trouble to obtain their favorite type of chert. Fine-grained and dense, the bluish gray fragments unearthed at Bluefish Caves bore no resemblance to local types of dull-black chert. In fact, after nearly twenty years of searching, Cinq-Mars has yet to track down the source of their stone anywhere in the Porcupine River basin. To stock up on this fine-grained chert, the hunters at Bluefish Caves likely journeyed to the northern mountains or traded whatever they could—tools, songs, knowledge—with other friendly bands. Cinq-Mars favors the latter possibility. "Survival here requires that you have alliances. Information in this environment is as important as tools."

But intriguing as these discoveries were, Cinq-Mars reserved his greatest vigilance for bone tools. And in 1983 while working in the laboratory sorting through bone scraps, he came across something hauntingly familiar: a large talon-shaped flake tool almost identical to those excavated a decade earlier along the Old Crow River. Encouraged, he returned to Bluefish a few months later with a small team of French colleagues. And as they labored quietly, someone called him over. Just above bedrock lay a foot-long chunk of mammoth bone scarred by percussive blows. "And right then and there it clicked," says Cinq-Mars. "The shape of the scar on that bone reminded me of the flake I'd picked up the winter before in the lab." Bundling the precious bone in his hand luggage, Cinq-Mars carted it back to Ottawa himself. Hurrying into the laboratory, he dug out the talon-shaped flake from the drawers and held it up to the scar. "It was a perfect match."

Team members reveled in the news. Unearthed from a high ridgetop cave, the flake tool could not have been splintered by river ice nor shattered by trampling animals around a waterhole. Nor did it reveal any gouging or scraping marks from carnivores' sharp teeth. Instead, a Beringian hunter had clearly struck it off from the mammoth bone core in a series of deliberate, sequential steps. The burning question was when. To pinpoint it, Cinq-Mars needed solid radiocarbon dates.

But, as luck would have it, the controversy long simmering around the Old Crow work was now about to boil over. In British Columbia, one of the continent's leading archaeometrists had just retested the now famous caribou-bone flesher, all that remained from Irving's original radiocarbon sample. Armed with more reliable methods of eliminating contaminants from ancient bone and powerful new equipment for counting the decay rate of radiocarbon—the atomic clock that ticks away in all organic material—Erle Nelson had come to a stunning new conclusion. The original dates were seriously in error: The famous flesher dated back a mere 1,350 years, a small blink of the eye in archaeological terms.

At once, critics descended on the northern Yukon work, scarcely able to conceal their glee. In his Ottawa laboratory, Cinq-Mars sat and bristled. To stave off doubters, he turned over testing of his key specimens to Nelson's laboratory. And with years of weary work at stake, he waited anxiously for the results. When the final set of dates rolled in, he heaved a sigh of quiet relief. By the archaeometrist's careful work, the mammoth-bone flake and core dated back some 23,500 years—to the bitterest cold of the last glaciation.

Today, as he leans back against a rugged cave wall, Cinq-Mars is convinced that Beringian hunters took brief shelter here from time to time over a period of some 15,000 years. "You can think of a small hunting party stopping in one of these caves for an afternoon, if it was a rainy day or a bad blizzard or a freak storm." And he firmly believes that the transients hammered out tools of bone there. Requiring no trips to distant mountain quarries, no exchange of valuable goods, bone lay as near to hand as the next large carcass. Eminently expendable, a bone flake could be rapped out in a moment and tossed away as soon as butchering was done. It was the medium of expediency, the plastic of the Paleolithic era.

✦   ✦   ✦

In a cavernous storage room half a world away in southern Ontario, Richard Harington marvels over the roan-colored remains of Ice Age giants. A tall, burly man with short brown hair and a quiet, retiring manner of speech, Harington is the curator of Quaternary zoology at the Canadian Museum of Nature in Ottawa. One of the world's foremost authorities on the fauna of eastern Beringia, the former wildlife biologist has spent the last three decades sifting through fossilized bone from the northern Yukon, identifying dozens of strange Ice Age species—from beavers as large as black bears to mammoths the size of African elephants.

For Harington, even now, the northern Yukon remains a land of mystery and paradox. Bitterly cold and windswept as it must have been at the height of the last glaciation, he says, this eastern fringe of Beringia harbored a strange abundance of life. Studies of fossil pollen preserved in Bluefish Caves, for example, reveal traces of a vast grassland that once blanketed the region. Woven with sagebrush and sedges and edged with water-loving dwarf willows, it bore little resemblance to any environment known on the earth today. And it clearly offered rich fare for animals. "I think the productivity of this steppe-like grassland was relatively high," says Harington, "certainly much higher than it is now."

And a host of large mammals were quick to take advantage. According to Harington's careful studies, more than twenty-five species of large grazing and browsing animals wandered the region. Along the Bluefish River, for example, tundra musk ox and woolly mammoths, their long tusks curving into the air, grazed low-lying willows, quietly stripping the branches. On drier ground, huge, long-horned steppe bison wallowed in the dust, while herds of pony-sized horses and sandy-colored antelope kicked up their heels in the cool northern winds. On the slopes above, caribou and Dall's sheep crisscrossed the high meadows, watching warily for predators.

Such abundance would surely have tempted Beringian hunters. "I think it would have been very attractive for humans," says Harington. And equipped as they likely were with lethal stone-tipped spears, humans were more than a match for most of this game. Among the trove of more than 10,000 bones exhumed from Bluefish Caves—the largest ever excavated from caves in northwestern North America—paleontologists identified nine species of large herbivores, meaty prey for hunters. Of these, caribou and mammoth were particularly plentiful.

But for all their weaponry and skill, Beringian hunters still had to exercise considerable caution: The grasslands were rife with dangerous rivals. The northern Yukon, for example, boasted the largest carnivore in Ice Age North America, an ursine giant known as the short-faced bear. Fleet-footed master of the high-speed chase, the short-faced bear combined the powerful jaws of a grizzly with the swiftness of a lion. Reaching more than 5 feet high at the shoulder, males tipped the scales at 1,500 pounds. "If one of these things had stood up on its hind legs," says Harington, "it would have been simple for it to dunk a basketball just standing there."

And other perils stalked the grasses at night. Under cover of darkness, prides of lions, similar to those roaming the Serengeti today, awakened in the tall grasses, ready to hunt. Elsewhere in the valleys, sleek scimitar cats stole through the brush. Distantly related to the better-known saber-toothed cat, the scimitars brandished a deadly set of curving serrated teeth. "They were like steak knives in a way," says Harington. "I think they were used for slashing either tendons or blood vessels. So these cats could just follow their prey as they bled along the trail."

Despite such fearsome rivals, humans prospered along the cold grasslands of eastern Beringia. They had, after all, millennia of experience to draw on. During the bitter cold of the last glaciation, which began some 115,000 years ago, much of Asia and Europe teemed with shaggy mammoths, bison, caribou, horses, and a host of other eastern Beringian species. For Asian hunters, the route to North America was a grassy one, paved with familiarity. "The mammoth fauna was pretty much of a likeness," marvels Harrington, "all the way from England to the Baillie Islands in the Northwest Territories."

✦   ✦   ✦

Just when Siberian hunters first followed caribou or mammoth east to Alaska, pitching camps in great rolling valleys that no human eyes had ever seen before, is a question that continues to haunt Cinq-Mars. On a warm summer night, as he sits in his tiny field laboratory in Old Crow taping crates of samples, he considers the question. Surrounded by maps, neatly boxed columns of sediment and bags of beach cobbles, he harbors no illusion that he has uncovered relics of the earliest humans in North America. Bluefish Caves, he says, merely prove that native hunters lived here at least 23,000 years ago. "Beringia," he smiles obliquely, reaching for a nearby tumbler of scotch, "had to be peopled earlier than that."

The evidence, he explains, lies in a tantalizing piece of research conducted by Richard Morlan, a colleague at the Canadian Museum of Civilization. A few years ago, Morlan dug out the Old Crow River collection of bone flakes and cores for a new round of radiocarbon tests. If natural agents such as river ice or carnivores had produced these flakes, reasoned Morlan, the bones would yield a random distribution of dates, for such forces had been at work throughout the Ice Age. If humans, however, had splintered off the flakes, the bones would date back only to the earliest time that hunters had lived in the Yukon. Morlan dispatched the collection to Nelson's laboratory, and waited. All the flakes and cores dated from 25,000 to 40,000 years ago, although the archaeometrist's methods permitted the accurate dating of samples up to 50,000 years in age. "All of a sudden," says Cinq-Mars, "there is this new added quality, this new figure popping up in the environment [40,000 years ago]. And all things being equal, I personally believe this agent to be *Homo*."

Indirect and slender as such evidence is, the stubborn researcher is convinced it deserves attention. And he believes the date is particularly significant, straddling as it does one of the most remarkable periods in Old World prehistory. Some 45,000 to 35,000 years ago, modern humans surged through Europe and parts of Asia; at the same time, indigenous bands of *Homo sapiens neanderthalensis*, or Neanderthals, vanished. Precisely what transpired between these two closely related peoples is a subject that tantalizes scholars. Some believe our modern human ancestors stormed out of an African homeland, vanquishing the Neanderthals of Europe and Asia with superior wit and technology. Others suggest that we evolved from several native populations—including the Neanderthals—in disparate parts of the world.

Regardless of our origins, nothing was ever the same again. "You've got tremendous quantities of change," says Cinq-Mars. In rock shelters across Europe, small bands of humans began turning out ingenious new weapons and tools, adorning themselves with animal-tooth pendants and mammoth-ivory beads and setting forth into remote regions never before colonized. It was at roughly this moment, for example, that seafaring bands of humans crossed the waters from Southeast Asia to Greater Australia. And it was at this period that Eurasian bands finally mastered survival in such frigid regions as southern Siberia. "Sites along the upper Yenisey River reflect an ability to cope in cold boreal or sub-boreal environments 35,000 to 40,000 years ago, or a bit more in some cases," says Cinq-Mars.

At that point, few barriers stood between Asian bands and the New World. Capable of fashioning warm clothing and winter shelters, they had learned to endure brutal subzero days and nights. Adept at hunting herd animals, they had mastered ways of feeding themselves in a harsh land. And the innate desire to see what lay beyond the next valley may have been just as much a part of their psyche as it is ours today. With each passing year, bands may have pushed a little farther north and east, sons extending their fathers' hunting grounds, grandsons still more, until at last they landed in a new world. "The arrival of human beings here," says Cinq-Mars, "is the logical step after human populations were capable of surviving in boreal, subarctic, or arctic environments. They could not but expand rapidly."

Exactly who these new North Americans were—modern humans or some archaic kin such as the Neanderthals—is still far from clear today. And what happened to these Siberian migrants when they landed in the New World is still open to speculation. While some bands likely staked out territory in eastern Beringia, giving rise eventually to the hunters of Bluefish Caves, others may well have continued their journey southward. Evidence of this ancient trek, however, remains scanty in North America. The best clues arise farther south. Along the coast of Chile, for example, American archaeologist Tom Dillehay has unearthed what appears to be an ancient campsite with three hearths dating as early as 40,000 years ago.

While Cinq-Mars would clearly welcome stronger proof of such an early passage, he is not overly troubled by its absence. It is entirely possible, he suggests, as he tapes shut the last of his wooden crates, that early travelers in southern latitudes met with a series of misfortunes that extinguished some and forced back others until conditions were more favorable. "In reality," he concludes, "it must have been a very fluctuating front. We're certainly aware of cases of aborted advances, and populations may have gone far beyond that main front and disappeared, never to be seen again."

✦   ✦   ✦

On the last evening of the field season, Cinq-Mars and I stand on the banks of the Porcupine River, watching the waters flow west toward the Bering Sea. At eleven at night, the sun still shines high in a bright blue sky. Motorboats rumble up and down the water, ferrying Gwich'in families to distant fishing camps. Pinching tobacco out along the fold of a cigarette paper, Cinq-Mars listens to the laughter of children playing in the distance. Behind us, a traditional northern flatbread, bannock, rises on the stove in the field laboratory, filling the air with the sweet warmth of a bakery.

For the past two days now, Cinq-Mars has been restless, his thoughts turned firmly to the moment when he can return south to his Quebec home and family. With each passing year, the graying archaeologist loses a little more of the youth, a little more of the physical strength that once made this work seem so easy. But for all his growing weariness, Cinq-Mars can't quit now: There is no one else to carry on the work. Irving has died, Morlan has moved on, and no younger researcher has appeared to inherit their mantle. With only one other archaeologist at work now in the entire northern Yukon, Cinq-Mars feels he has no choice but to soldier on.

And better than anyone else, he knows the burden of proof his work must eventually shoulder. No loose ends can be left to spark doubt, as other researchers have ruefully discovered. Seventy years ago, for example, North America's leading archaeologists were convinced that Eurasians had first landed in the New World well after the last ice sheets had retreated. "As to the antiquity of the Indian himself," sniffed Aleš Hrdlička, curator of physical anthropology at the Smithsonian's United States National Museum, "that cannot be very great" (Gardener 1986). Researchers who questioned this article of faith risked professional censure. But a few mavericks persisted, and in 1927, a small team unearthed a dazzling piece of evidence in New Mexico: a stone spearpoint embedded near the ribs of an Ice Age bison. It was enough to convince most professionals, but a few skeptics still remained. Hrdlička himself, for example, died unrepentant.

So for Cinq-Mars, the fieldwork goes on. He is still mustering his case, making new maps, drilling new core samples, dating the demise of glacial lakes. And he is still scouring the countryside, searching for early winter camps, kill sites, and quarries, and the tantalizing evidence that remains forever just out of reach. And as I gaze out on the river, I can tell that he will never be satisfied, never done. He looks at me and smiles. "A friend of mine told me that, too," he admits finally, his tone wistful. "He told me, 'It's much too hard. You and I won't live long enough to find all the things you hope to find.'" He pauses and looks back out to the river. "He's probably right."

2

ULTRAMARINE
Eel Point, California

All excess brings trouble to mankind.

—PLAUTUS

Nobody knows better than Mark Raab what a great fishing spot this is. Perched on the rugged cape of a remote island some sixty miles from civilization and the southern California mainland, the sinewy researcher breathes in the salty air and smiles. Along the far shore of the bay, straw-colored terraces descend in giant, rounded steps to the sea. Ribbons of rusty-orange kelp bob in the waves. Raab turns and picks his way back to the ridge, propping his fishing rod on the rocks. In the far distance, sea lions bark like hungry dogs. A pelican sweeps overhead, its brown wings beating against the breeze. Raab listens a moment, then picks out a mass of limp silver from a bucket of squid.

Wiry and weathered, with the broad shoulders of a man who has spent much time in the water, Raab has seen for himself just how generous the sea here can be. For nearly a week, he and a team of experts have been excavating nearby dunes strewn with the fishing trophies of an ancient and mysterious culture of marine hunter-gatherers. Ranging over nearly five acres, the sands of Eel Point resemble the refuse of a fine

33

seafood restaurant. Riddled with tons of lustrous seashells and thousands of bones of shark, barracuda, moray eel, rockfish, sheephead, kelp bass, mackerel, and other ocean creatures, the largest heaps of debris stand nearly 16 feet high. Raab shakes his head. "There's no doubt about it," he says finally, "these people were really going to town."

After another day of sifting through this strange boneyard, he and a handful of his colleagues have come here tonight to try their own luck. Skewering a slice of squid to his hook, Raab, an authority on the prehistory of the California coast, saunters back to the edge of the rocks. With his eye on the kelp beds, he casts his line. In the dense tangle of amber fronds below, opaleye, fringehead, garibaldi, and hundreds of other species prowl; in the sandy clearings, flounder, halibut, and turbot flourish. This small bay is one of the richest fishing grounds on the island. But after nearly two hours of effort tonight, Raab has yet to land even a sea perch. And his four associates are faring little better. Standing on the other side of the rocks, Bill Howard, a determined, no-nonsense field archaeologist in his late fifties, turns and points sheepishly to a small tidal pool on a ledge below. Finning furtively along the bottom is the sole catch of the day—a 10-inch-long kelpfish too small to keep.

But for the five dusty anglers, such evenings only whet their curiosity about a region long ignored by their colleagues. For years, North American prehistorians took a dim view of coastal dwellers. Little impressed by the simple stone tools unearthed from shore-bound camps in California, early researchers came to see these tribes as simple beachcombers who spent their days dawdling along shores and lazily digging clams. The overall portrait was less than flattering. "The manner of procuring the essentials of life by collecting shells," noted renowned coastal archaeologist Max Uhle sternly in 1907, "in itself indicates a low form of human existence" (Raab 1994). In all likelihood, suggested researchers, wandering tribes had settled along the Pacific coast relatively late, after all choice inland territories had been claimed by more vigorous cultures.

But studies by a small band of specialists on the remote southern Channel Islands show just how wrong Uhle and his associates were. Far from being Johnny-come-latelies, these islanders numbered among the earliest colonists of California. Braving strong currents and gusty winds, they soon mastered the waves there, quickly assuming the mantle of top marine predator. Armed with little more than stealth, they slaughtered sleek sea lions larger than themselves and feasted on the fat. Fashioning hooks, lines, and other fishing gear, they prowled the kelp beds, one of the world's richest ecosystems. And when times were right, these marine adventurers landed one of the swiftest and most agile animals in the ocean—dolphins. "They weren't just no-brainers rooting around in the surf," says Raab.

Possessing a knowledge of the ocean that would put many modern marine scientists to shame, they thrived on these small islands, eventually settling down and building houses much as early farmers did elsewhere. And over time, they began plundering the sea. Cleverly preying on the weaknesses of fish, mammal, and bird, they wiped out certain stocks and drove other key predators to the edge of extinction, imperiling an entire ecosystem. "They were anything but wise conservators," notes Raab, shaking his head. "Like human beings anywhere, if they had a choice between ideology and eating, they picked eating. And they extirpated species left and right."

Deeply curious about this new work, I have joined Raab and his colleagues in the field on San Clemente Island. Situated sixty miles off the coast of San Diego, at the far southern end of the Santa Barbara Channel, San Clemente belongs to the United States government. Set aside in 1934 as a naval reservation and closed to the public, it has escaped the schemes of southern California land developers, remaining largely wild. Along its sixty square miles lie an estimated 7,500 prehistoric sites, one of the highest concentrations anywhere in western North America. Eager to sift through refuse of the island's oldest known inhabitants, Raab and close collaborator Andy Yatsko, a civilian staff archaeologist with the

Navy, have launched a major excavation at Eel Point. Negotiating stacks of military paperwork on everything from vehicles to barrack accommodations, they have flown a team of professional archaeologists to the island.

And on an early Saturday morning in August, a tousled crew gathers for breakfast in the island mess hall. Dressed in rumpled blue jeans and dirt-smudged T-shirts, experts on subjects as diverse as marine mammals and shell fishhooks jostle for space along a row of gleaming toasters. Comparing notes on the comfortable barracks and the alien rules and regulations that govern every aspect of life here ("please don't talk about anything confidential," warns one hallway sign, "the phones are monitored at all time"), they fill their cups with muddy coffee. Weaving past groups of young men in combat fatigues and navy blues, they trickle down to the empty tables at the far end of the room. Along the wall-length picture window, neighboring Santa Catalina Island rises in the distance from a meringue of white cloud.

Bringing up the rear, Raab slides into an empty chair. A slender man with neatly chiseled features, high cheekbones, and closely cropped wavy hair, he tucks away his sunglasses. Dressed this morning in a gray sweatshirt, mottled combat fatigues, and high-laced boots, Raab looks more like an air force colonel than an archaeologist. But at age fifty, the sociable researcher clearly lives, eats, and breathes prehistory. Surrounded by like-minded souls—including his dark-haired wife and colleague Ginger Bradford—he holds the floor easily, deftly steering the conversation as it winds from the transexuality of particular kelp-bed fish to the ease of hunting certain extinct puffins. ("These birds had a habit of gorging themselves on floating carcasses of whales until they could no longer fly," he observes, shaking his head. "They ate fat.")

Listening to Raab on a roll is a little like turning on the Discovery Channel. And yet the ocean didn't always rivet his attention. Born and raised just outside San Diego, Raab began his academic career in the deserts of the American Southwest, surveying and digging prehistoric sites of the maize-farming Hohokam people. With a doctoral degree from

Arizona State University, he pushed east to Arkansas and Texas, making a name for himself as an expert on interactions between prehistoric humans and their environments. But in the mid-1980s, a troubled divorce sent his life spinning. Returning west, he accepted a job at California State University in Northridge. The Channel Islands soon beckoned. At Naval Air Station North Island in San Diego, Yatsko was casting around for a collaborator to embark on a major research program at San Clemente.

This morning, with a full day ahead in the field, the two men are anxious to get down to business. Rousing the crew, they dart out the door to a parking lot lined with identical white vans. Coffee in hand, I fold into a backseat behind Raab and peer out the window as we barrel past a warren of anonymous-looking trailers and a row of giant satellite dishes. A test range for cruise missiles and a training ground for antiterrorist commandos and other naval troops, San Clemente possesses a surreal air. Along one shrub-dotted knoll, a sign welcomes travelers to San Clemente National Forest. Along another, a simulated missile base—complete down to wooden cutout missiles—fades in the sun like the set of a Hollywood movie.

But as we turn down the island's western flanks, the veneer of military life disappears. An austere wilderness of rock and desert scrub opens up ahead of us. Along the upper edges of the terraces, a red-tailed hawk rides the thermals; on the slopes below, lizards scuttle for shade in patches of spiny cactus. Twisting around in his seat, Raab explains that the island was not always so desolate. When the first American surveyors landed here in the mid-nineteenth century, he says, they wandered up slopes of waving grasses and past thickets of hibiscuslike lavatera, oak, and other trees. But ravenous livestock nearly stripped the land bare in later years—until the Navy put an end to all such grazing. "The island was badly ravaged," says Raab, shaking his head.

Even at its most verdant, however, San Clemente never harbored much terrestrial game—no deer, for example, or wild boar. But its shores teemed with life, and as we wind down the slope, my eyes are drawn to the crooked finger of land ahead—Eel Point. Drawing to a stop beside the team's small field camp, we wriggle out from the van. Raab grabs his pack from the back and heads up the hill. At nine in the morning, only a smear of white cloud lingers on the horizon; the sea stretches out clear and blue below. But it is not the far view that fascinates me most. On the bare ground beneath our feet, countless fragments of lustrous pink shell and mother-of-pearl shimmer from the sand.

On the hilltop, crew members raise a flapping plastic canopy over the deepest of two pits. Raab ducks down the ladder. Nearly 8 feet deep and layered in tawny bands of sand, shell, and bone, this pit was first opened a decade or so ago by Clement Meighan and students from the University of California in Los Angeles. A prominent coastal archaeologist, Meighan had become intrigued by the size and depth of these refuse heaps, which suggested great antiquity. Troweling down through the exquisitely preserved layers, he and his crew members gathered up not only stone tools, shell fishhooks, and other human handiwork, but thousands of tiny fragments of fish bone for later identification and study.

But it was the team's series of radiocarbon dates that really stirred researchers' imaginations. While native bands had clearly frequented Eel Point as recently as the eleventh century A.D., some people had arrived here much, much earlier. Indeed, if the earliest radiocarbon date was right—and critics soon raised serious doubts—a small band of nomads camped briefly along this rocky point 10,800 years ago, at the end of the last Ice Age. Coastal researchers shook their heads in wonderment. Did voyagers really reach this remote marine outpost of California at almost the same time as hunter-gatherers first colonized mainland valleys some 11,000 years ago?

The question was rich in implication. Unlike other islands farther north along the coast, San Clemente had never been part of the mainland. To reach its shores even by island-hopping, early voyagers had crossed forty miles of windblown ocean in small watercraft such as reed rafts or dugout canoes—no easy matter. "Anybody who's ever been out in a

View of Eel Point. (Courtesy of the author.)

small boat in these waters," says Raab, "knows it takes a pretty fair degree of seamanship to survive here." And these early mariners seemed a breed apart from the mainlanders, possessing none of the finely made throwing darts and other weaponry favored by terrestrial hunters. At the University of California, Meighan wondered whether people here had descended directly from Asian coastal cultures. Perhaps Old World mariners had paddled eastward along the rim of the Pacific Ocean during the late Ice Age, eventually migrating down the coast of North America.

Evidence, however, remained scarce. Rising sea levels at the end of the Ice Age inundated large stretches of shoreline along the West Coast; highways and housing subdivisions obliterate much of what remains. To seek out new data, Raab and Yatsko have returned to Eel Point. By expanding previous excavations and combing the site for potentially older deposits, the two men hope to firmly date the site's lowest and most contentious layer and to conduct a detailed study of human cultural evolution here over 10,000 years. Time is running short, however. The team has permission for just another

ten days of work here. Clambering out of the pit, Raab shakes
his head. "Time is pressing," he says. "And it just takes so long
to get down to depth."

✦   ✦   ✦

Squinting in the sun, Judy Porcasi gives the screen a last hard
shake, sending flakes of mother-of-pearl shimmering to the
ground. For the past few hours, team members have been
moving through a layer sulfurous with the smell of death.
Loaded with shell and reddish-colored bone, the sediments
are a kind of bouillabaisse in dried form. Five people are now
working the screens furiously: Porcasi couldn't be happier. A
doctoral student in zooarchaeology, the diminutive faunal
expert has plucked out hundreds of exquisitely preserved
animal remains—triangular shark teeth, smooth mahogany-
colored fish ribs, sturdy seabird beaks.

But it is the big splinters that light Porcasi's smile. Pluck-
ing out three or four from her screen, she gently brushes off
the sand. Rolling them over in her hand, one by one, she studies them intently through her pop-bottle-thick glasses, searching for certain characteristic bumps and depressions that will
help her identify the species or genera. Satisfied finally, she
tucks them into a plastic tray overflowing with similar fragments. Glancing over at Raab, she beams. "Dolphin."

This is, as everyone agrees, a strange and wonderful layer.
Paved with bones and shell, it looks very much like the refuse
of a people living very well off the sea. Indeed, rubbish piled up
so thick and fast here that it was rapidly buried, leaving little
time for decay. But what fascinates Raab and Porcasi most is
the windfall of dolphin bone. Early prehistoric peoples in California rarely feasted on dolphin meat. Still, both scientists have
seen something much like this layer once before—on neighboring Santa Catalina Island to the north. "The kinds of species
that are here, the density of bone, the degree of preservation is
very much like what we saw at Little Harbor," says Raab.

Perched, like Eel Point, on a western shore, Little Harbor
has been the subject of professional curiosity for nearly forty

years now. First dug by Meighan in the early 1950s, the refuse heaps, or middens, were so choked with shell and butchered carcasses that frustrated crew members soon abandoned screening, picking out only the largest bones by hand. Faunal experts poring over the collection were amazed. Four out of every five mammal bones belonged to *Cetacea,* the family containing both dolphins and porpoises. Most of the rest came from seals and sea lions. Little Harbor seemed to be in a class by itself, a mysterious exception to prehistoric coastal life. "The animals were a real stumper," says Raab. "What the hell were these people doing, eating dolphins?"

Baffled, some researchers tried to ignore Little Harbor. But Raab was fascinated. After poring over the scientific literature, he suspected that the ocean itself held some explanation. Some years back, oceanographer Nicklas Pisias had published a key paper on marine temperatures in the region. By counting tiny heat-sensitive animals in seafloor sediments, Pisias had charted a jagged line of winter water temperatures over the past 8,000 years. Ranging as low as 53°F and as high as 75°F, these radical temperature swings—triggered by great global shifts in ocean circulation—undoubtedly affected animal life in the ocean.

Keen to put the theory to a test, Raab decided to excavate. Mustering a team of students and associates, he arrived on Santa Catalina in 1991, laying out three small excavation units. Before long, team members were scooping out handfuls of bone from the famous ashy-gray layer. "It was just so rich," marvels Raab. Back at Northridge, team members pored over the finds: The famous dolphin strata dated back some 5,200 years—to the beginning of an ancient marine hot spell. According to Pisias's chart, winter water temperatures in the region had soared from 57 to 66°F. And summer temperatures likely kept pace, rocketing from 66 to 78°F.

Team members were baffled. Such sultry waters should have decimated marine life. While studying the effects of El Niño currents, marine botanists had discovered that tropical warmth kills giant brown algae—the most important kelp-bed species in the region. As ocean temperatures crest above 68°F, nutrient levels fall. After just two weeks of such warmth, brown algae begins to wither—a death knell for the creatures depending on it. But at Little Harbor, where such tropical temperatures reigned for decades in summer, there was no sign of marine famine. Indeed, it looked like a bumper crop.

Had Pisias erred in his chart? The midden itself was larded with clues. Some 5,200 years ago, people at Little Harbor had landed great catches of warm-water-loving tuna. Indeed 65 percent of all fish bones unearthed in the refuse belonged to species of tuna. And the hunters at Little Harbor had relished another heat-seeking animal, too. Among the more than 1,400 dolphin bones collected during the dig, Porcasi identified four species that roam California waters today: the common, white-sided, bottle-nosed, and northern right-whale dolphins. But some fragments clearly belonged to a more exotic, warm-water species—the blue dolphin, or *Stenella coeruleoalba*, that threads the tropical and subtropical waters of Mexico today.

Clearly, Santa Catalina waters were much warmer 5,200 years ago than they are now. And Raab now believes that the sheer length of this heat wave proved a saving grace. As the canopy of giant brown algae shriveled, other kelp species in the understory likely blossomed in the new patches of light. Far from wreaking havoc, he now suggests, warm water "supercharges the environment. It brings tuna and other warm-water pelagic species from the south, and when those species are here in large numbers, the large predators like dolphins and sea lions are here, too. The food chain changes because all these predators are coming in and working the kelp beds. And of course the top predator in the food chain, *Homo sapiens,* is out working the food chain too."

Just how hunters slew the sleek aquatic predators—sea lions weighing from 110 to 650 pounds, dolphins tipping the scales between 150 and 600 pounds—remains unclear. It is quite likely, however, that small raiding parties plundered sea-lion rookeries on land, driving mothers and cubs away from the water and clubbing them to death. But dolphins would have required very different measures. Quite possibly, suggests Raab, hunters profited from the animals' peculiar traveling habits. As commercial fishers along this coast have long known, some dolphins—including *Stenella coeruleoalba*—accompany large schools of tuna. Perhaps prehistoric islanders set nets for tuna in a submarine canyon at Little Harbor, occasionally hauling in dolphins instead.

But on this salty summer afternoon at Eel Point, as Porcasi picks out yet more dolphin bone from her screen, she wonders whether people here went to far greater and more perilous lengths. Opening up a small plastic vial, Porcasi shakes out a very new find: a slender, thumb-length piece of bone, notched at one end. It looks very much like the barbs that later Channel Islanders lashed to harpoons for spearing swordfish, seals, and sea lions. Porcasi holds it out for my inspection. At Little Harbor, no one has ever uncovered any trace of these harpoons. "There's been a lot of talk about finding them," she says with a broad smile, "because that would mean they were going to sea and hunting sea mammals."

✦　✦　✦

In the silvery light of the slide projector, I lean forward in the couch, staring up at a white sheet tacked to the wall of the field laboratory. It's just after nine on a Saturday night on San Clemente, and Raab, Yatsko, and their associates have dispensed with the customary rounds of cold beer in the military bar. Freshly showered and decked out in clean clothes, team members drape over tables and perch on sagging chesterfields, taking in the evening's entertainment. On the wrinkled screen looms the photograph of a 5,000-year-old ruin that Yatsko and a small team discovered not far from where we sit.

To be exact, the ruin consists of a rough circular floor the color of gray chalk. And it is one of many: Over the past few years, team members have mapped or partially excavated seventeen other similar hollows at the Nursery site (named by its discoverers after a nearby nursery). In all likelihood, says Raab, the floor once formed part of a large conical dwelling that owed much to the water. Sea mammal hides or seagrass mats probably formed the outer wall. The bones of a leviathan served for the frame. "See right here?" he asks, walking over to the sheet and pointing to a series of dark pits along the edge of the floor. "These are postholes at the periphery of the floor. And in this one, we found the butt of a whale rib. Whale ribs were once arcing in toward the center."

Just how islanders acquired these bones is far from clear, but Raab seriously doubts that people here ever risked their lives by whaling. The huge animals are often spied offshore here, and their carcasses wash up frequently: In 1989 alone, two blue whales and one minke whale drifted in dead. But while nature likely supplied the building materials, people here still had their work cut out for them. The shoulder blade or jawbone of a large whale can weigh several hundred pounds: To raise a building at the Nursery site, people had to haul such deadweight more than a mile from shore and 700 feet above sea level.

Clearly, they had something more in mind than an overnight camp. Indeed, Raab now believes that these 5,000-year-old whalebone lodges signify the beginnings of settled life on the island. And he is convinced that inhabitants gave up their old ways with great reluctance. "We think in our society that what we would like to do is settle down somewhere," he notes, "that sedentism is much better than mobility." But some theorists, such as Lewis Binford, suggest that wanderlust was once the wellspring of survival. If food supplies failed in one place, hunter-gatherers could swiftly head off to the next. "And when people are moving around," says Raab, "they are reconnoitering the environment and sharing information with adjacent bands. Survival is an information network based fundamentally on mobility."

But around 3000 B.C., all that began to change. Amply fed by the warm ocean waters, human populations soared. Hedged increasingly by neighbors, people were no longer free to plunder all the shellfish at one spot and quickly paddle off to another. Someone else was already there. So, like many late Paleolithic peoples in the Old World, islanders were forced to make do in a smaller territory. In the Middle East, wandering bands solved the problem by taking up agriculture, sowing and reaping cereal grains. People on San Clemente, however, turned to a very different remedy—fishing. "It's really the only economic system that could be intensified," says Raab. By devising sturdier boats and more elaborate gear and by fishing a wider range of coastal habitats, islanders could harvest more food from the sea.

Certainly they began laboring on new types of tackle. For generations, people in these parts relied on a deceptively simple-looking piece of tackle known as the gorge. Shaped like a small needle but sharpened at both ends, the gorge may have served a variety of purposes. Tied to the end of a line, it could have acted as a hook, toggling and wedging in the animal's gullet. Or it may have been part of a fish spear carried underwater, for evidence suggests that the islanders were practiced divers. As Raab points out, some human remains unearthed on San Clemente reveal a condition of the inner ear known as auditory exostosis, caused by repeated diving and swimming in cold water.

But some 4,700 years ago, bands in the region began turning out a new type of tackle. Taking silvery abalone shell as a raw material, they set to work crafting circular fishhooks. Roughly the size of an American quarter and the shape of an exaggerated crescent moon, the circular shell hook was perfectly suited to fishing in deeper rocky reefs: It did not snag easily. Moreover, its shiny iridescence, so similar to the glistening scales on some fish, proved hopelessly seductive. Almost at once, islanders began landing record catches: One study shows that fishing productivity soared tenfold at Eel Point after the appearance of these hooks.

And they didn't stop there. In the darkened room, Raab clicks the remote control. The photograph of a woven seagrass pouch and a tumble of fishing gear appears on the wrinkled sheet. The audience stares in silence. "You see all this stuff?" asks Raab with a flourish. "It's a fishing kit that was buried with somebody at the Nursery site." Found beside small soapstone carvings of killer whales, the 1,400-year-old pouch brims with the intricate tools of a fisher's trade—bone gorges, circular shell hooks, net spacers, weights, rasps for sharpening hooks, scaling scrapers, stone knives, and containers of beach tar for repairing equipment.

To modern North American eyes, this elaborate kit seems the embodiment of progress; the tools are plentiful, the technology ingenious. But Raab sees matters differently. Only when starvation threatened, only when people had been hammering away at scarce marine resources for thousands of years, did bands turn wholeheartedly to fishing and the laborious technology involved. "From this point of view, there's really no such thing as a natural motive towards progress," he concludes. "It really suggests that necessity is the mother of invention and that human beings come up with these things because they get into a problem."

✦   ✦   ✦

In the early seventeenth century, an adventuresome Spanish chronicler, Father Antonio de la Ascensión, penned a brief account of his sojourn on the Channel Islands. Landing on remote Santa Catalina in late November, 1602, the young friar was soon charmed by island life. The women, dressed in robes of sealskin, were beautiful and modest; the homes, covered with woven rushes that reminded de la Ascensión of Moorish mats, were comfortable. Food, in the form of native root vegetables and fish, abounded. But what seemed to capture the friar's fancy most was the dexterous skill of the men, who sliced through the waves in sturdy plank canoes. "They paddle on one side and the other in such unison and concert that they go flying," he marveled (Wagner 1966).

While de la Ascensión and the Spanish who followed proved the ultimate undoing of the islanders, the two cultures had more in common than is generally credited. Both peoples lived on intimate terms with the sea, maritime to the bone, and both fished with an almost insatiable hunger. To meet the staggering demand for seafood in Catholic Spain during the fifteenth century, Spanish Basque fishing boats scoured waters as far west as Newfoundland. And on the remote Channel

A 1,400-year-old "tackle box" from the Nursery site on San Clemente Island. The most complete kit of its kind ever found, the pouch held more than eighty fishing accessories: fishhooks, net spacers, drills, scaling scrapers, and knives. (Courtesy of the University of California, Los Angeles.)

Islands, inhabitants rifled the sea so thoroughly that they nearly brought an entire ecosystem to its knees.

The first clues to this ancient destruction came to light in the mid-1980s, as team members from the University of California at Los Angeles burrowed down through the sand at Eel Point, striking a layer paved exclusively with remains of purple sea urchins. A small marine animal shaped like a pincushion with long, sturdy, radiating spines, the purple sea urchin feeds on kelp fronds along the seafloor. Awkward to handle and seldom reaching sizes larger than an apple, these creatures make an unlikely staple (although patrons of Japanese sushi bars fancy the roe as a delicacy). What induced islanders to consume such massive quantities a millennium ago?

While puzzling over this question, faunal analyst Roy Salls remembered reading about similar layers in historic camps on the Aleutian Islands, just off the western coast of Alaska. In the nineteenth century, Aleut hunters took up a disastrous trade, selling the rich pelts of local sea otters to Russian and American buyers. The slaughter soon brought about ecological disaster. As the sea otters disappeared, populations of their favored prey—sea urchins—exploded. Before long, a plague of the spiny creatures blanketed the seafloor, mowing down entire kelp forests and evicting all of their animal life.

Had a similar catastrophe unfolded at Eel Point? A doctoral student in zooarchaeology and an experienced skin diver, Salls knew that one prominent species of fish, the California sheephead, specialized in dispatching sea urchins. Outfitted with thick crushing plates in its throat, the sheephead could consume the prickly creatures with impunity. And it clearly kept the hoards in check. During experiments conducted on San Nicholas Island to the northwest, divers removed all sheephead from a small nearshore area: Twelve months later, sea urchin populations had climbed by 25 percent. "They concluded that sheephead in this environment were a keystone predator," says Raab.

Moreover, prehistoric people on San Clemente had been very fond of sheephead. Weighing up to 37 pounds in times past, it was one of the largest fish in the nearshore waters. And as a solitary, territorial species, it struck even at unbaited hooks. Masters of opportunity, islanders had targeted them. In his studies of Eel Point and three other sites on San Clemente, Salls discovered that sheephead accounted for between half and three-quarters of all identifiable fish bone. And at Eel Point, the landed fish got smaller and smaller in size over the centuries—a clear sign of overfishing. "They were so intensively hitting these fish that they were destabilizing the nearshore ecosystem," says Raab.

While kelp forests eventually recolonized these regions, the islanders must have been horrified. Still they were no strangers to excess. Raab's recent research shows, for example, that islanders wiped out all the large black abalone from local tidal pools. And Porcasi's studies suggest that they literally ravaged nearby seabird colonies: One species of albatross suffered a particularly hard time as it hatched and reared its young on land. Large and ungainly, it struggled to take to the air when a predator appeared. "There's no question that these birds would be very vulnerable to attack by humans," says Raab. "It looks like people were just nailing them."

To the careful researcher, the conclusions are now inescapable. "The evidence on this island shows that any species that these people could get their hands on—if it were vulnerable—suffered. It's not an attack on Indians. It's a statement about human beings in all times and all places. I think we are so disappointed by ourselves, about what we as a culture have done to the environment, we would like to think that someone has been more responsible. We want a moral example and Indians fit the bill."

✦   ✦   ✦

It's a cold, leaden morning in December. Outside my office window in downtown Vancouver, rain slants down in great sheets, drenching to the skin those waiting for the light. The golden warmth of southern California seems a world away right now. But a letter from Raab has arrived this morning. The new radiocarbon dates for Eel Point are now in. The sprawling seaside camp, it transpires, is almost two millennia younger than earlier researchers had supposed. It dates back to 7000 B.C.

By then, the glaciers of North America were in full retreat. Greenness was returning to the land and sea levels were rising, as small bands of migrants scattered across the length and breadth of North America. Those stepping onto the shores of Eel Point in these early times were clearly transients, Raab explains, as we talk on the phone. Hit-and-run artists, they made the most of coastal life—gathering shellfish, hunting sea mammals and seabirds, and doing a little fishing—before moving on. "There's a bit of everything in those lowest layers," Raab says.

Just who they were and where they came from remains a stubborn, unyielding mystery. Raab, for one, is no longer so certain that terrestrial hunters and their families arrived in the California interior some 11,000 years ago. Many of the early dates, he says, are based only on archaeologists' age estimates for certain types of stone weaponry. Radiocarbon test results are rare, for materials like charcoal, shell, and bone seldom escape decay in these moister sites. In the absence of solid dates, Raab keeps an open mind. "It may be that sites on the islands and the coast are as old as anything in the interior."

As I sit back in my chair later, thinking about his words, I try to imagine Eel Point, its rocky black ridge slick with waves. In the morning mist, a small boat bobs along the horizon; another slides into shore. A few people disembark, clambering up the beach as they listen to a sea lion roaring in the distance. Were they restless descendants of big-game hunters from the mainland? Or were they Asian mariners who had journeyed down thousands of miles of coastline, shaking their heads in wonder at the great ice-choked rivers, the mist-covered fjords, the empty cobble beaches?

Nobody knows. No one may ever know. Eel Point is silent.

3

THE RAPTURE
The Lower Pecos, Texas

All art worthy of the name is religious.

—HENRI MATISSE

First there's the land itself, with its menacing sweep and its rolling thunder of names: Big Satan Canyon, Devils River, Dead Man's Canyon, Frightful Cave, Mystic Shelter, Sorcerer's Cave. Then there's the malice of nature, where rattlesnakes wind through the dust and needle-sharp spines turn every shrub and strand of greenery into a particular form of torment: catclaw, horsecrippler, bayonet plant, crucifixion thorn. And finally there's the lingering presence of death—the carrion birds circling aimlessly over the canyon rim, the skeleton of a sheep whitening at a water hole. To the early Spanish settlers, who came to dread this desolate sweep, the lower Pecos River was part of the great *despoblado*, the uninhabited zone: To those who passed through later, it was an earthly vision of hell.

I have come to this southern fringe of Texas on an improbable journey—to see great galleries of art painted on cliff and cave walls more than 3,000 years ago. Strewn liberally along a maze of canyons carved along the northeastern end of the Chihuahuan desert, the strange teeming murals of birds,

panthers, snakes, and shamans constitute a little-known treasure, one of North America's oldest, largest, and most important collections of ritual art. To track down and record the
long-lost masterpieces, rock-art expert Solveig Turpin and a
small ragtag crew of graduate students and friends have spent
more than a decade combing this thorny wilderness. Giving
up weekends and holidays to crawl across sheer mountain
ledges and drop down stygian sinkholes, they are racing
against time to photograph and record the fragile murals before they fade from sight.

It is hard, sweaty, thankless work, and Turpin, a frank,
forthright woman in her late fifties with long, graying hair
swept back in a braid, isn't getting any younger. "The thing is,"
she explains ruefully, squinting into the sun, "we don't have
any money or any systematic big way to do this, as you would
a commercial activity." Relegated to the far fringes of archaeological research, where amateurs and hobbyists generally
roam, rock art seldom attracts serious professional attention.
But Turpin, the headstrong associate director of the Texas
Archeological Research Laboratory at the University of Texas
in Austin, is accustomed to breaking her own trails. Convinced the isolated paintings offer clues to a powerful ancient
religion that once blanketed the New World, she has taken on
the research as a personal labor of love.

This week, she and longtime colleague Jim Zintgraff, a
rock-art photographer from San Antonio, have set aside field
time to take me and two visiting researchers to see half a
dozen of the finest galleries. On this gentle March evening,
there are nine of us camped along the rocky brim of the Pecos
River canyon, our tents flapping gently in the breeze. Below
us, unseen in the folds of limestone, the Pecos rolls on silently
to the Rio Grande, just a mile or so away; in the distance, the
mountains of Mexico rise above the horizon like a band of
smoky-gray onyx. As we sit companionably around the campfire, watching darkness fall, the conversation returns once
again to the ancient paintings. In the flickering firelight,
Turpin recalls with a smile how she once vowed to turn away
from the temptation to interpret the puzzling figures. "They

tease me a lot about that now, the guys," she admits, her husky voice edged with laughter. "I said I wasn't going to deal with it, it's too fantastic, and I'm a scientist."

But how could she resist? For decades now, archaeologists have yearned to see into the minds and mysterious inner lives of the early people who called North America home. The passage of time and the relentless processes of decay, however, have greatly hindered such studies; little is left to attest to the spiritual and intellectual lives of ancient hunter-gatherers. After centuries of exposure, delicate ceremonial offerings, musical instruments, and ritual robes have long since crumbled to dust. And songs, dances, and mythologies have vanished into the thin, unforgiving air. Only scattered panels of rock art, long dismissed by most professional researchers as indecipherable and undatable, hint at a richer life.

Now the doors of perception are slowly opening. By scraping tiny traces of paint from caves along the confluence of the Pecos and Devils Rivers and the Rio Grande, an area popularly known as the Lower Pecos, physicists have experimentally dated the earliest style of art to some 3,000 to 4,200 years ago. And by gleaning clues from ethnographic studies of disparate modern and historic cultures, Turpin and her colleagues have finally begun cracking the millennia-old codes of metaphor and symbol. The earliest panels, they now suggest, were painted by ancient shamans—a mystical elite who served their followers by journeying to the otherworld to battle and commune with supernatural forces.

Moreover, the shamans of the Lower Pecos were adept at a particular form of this communion. To transcend the world of the flesh, suggests Carolyn Boyd, a doctoral student at Texas A&M University in College Station, they likely collected and consumed the world's oldest known hallucinogens. In altered states of consciousness, they wrestled with gods and spirits, conceiving strange visions they later recorded on rocky walls. For Boyd and others, the studies are shedding critical new light on the past. "We're finally getting to see into some part of these people's life that we never thought we would see," she says.

Eager for a glimpse into these mysteries, I brace myself next morning as we bounce over the water on the way to Panther Cave, spray lashing against the hull of our flat-bottomed boat. Ahead of us, like a muddy brown highway, the Rio Grande flows, cool and inviting, past canyon walls stacked with brilliant green cactus and brazen scarlet flowers. Along cane-littered banks, a lone heron rises from the shore in a graceful arc, wings almost touching the water; downstream, a flock of white pelicans dawdles contentedly on a sandbar. Impounded in the late 1960s to water a parched land, this stretch of the Rio Grande, known as Amistad Reservoir, now flows over river terraces where stands of willow, walnut, and pecan recently stood. But the past is not easily erased. Here and there, branches of drowned trees reach out like blackened fingers from the water.

Pushing back the hood of her cherry-red poncho, Turpin scours the upper cliffs for familiar landmarks, clearly in her element. With a smile full of crooked teeth and a flair for the dramatic, she points out the cairns that mark four Indian burials ("I always wanted to see what's under 'em") and a side

View of one of the many cave entrances in the Lower Pecos. (Copyright Robert W. Parvin.)

canyon that now protects an endangered species of pistachio, and in between she relates the short calamitous history of ranching in the region. "You know what they say about sheep in this country," she concludes with an ironic grin. "They're born looking for a place to die."

A warm, willful woman with an abiding love for this land, Turpin first arrived in the Lower Pecos in the late 1970s. A recently divorced mother of five and a doctoral student in anthropology, she had been hired to help map archaeological sites along the fence line of the newly created Seminole Canyon State Historical Park. For one born and raised in Minnesota, the Lower Pecos was an alien world, but she was determined to learn. Thrashing through the spiny brush and cooling off fully clothed in the local sheep troughs, she and fellow team members tracked down forty-eight new rock-art sites over the next two years in Seminole Canyon—doubling the previously known number. It was a personal testament to their tenacity, but it worried Turpin to no end. "We said, this was the area that had been the most studied in the whole Lower Pecos. So if this was the case here, what must it be like where nobody's been?"

Striking out on her own, Turpin began wringing reluctant permission from ranchers to search for sites on private lands. And as she clambered up and down rugged cliffs from Ozona, Texas, in the north to Musquiz, Mexico, in the south, she developed an enduring appreciation for those who had gone before. Along the deeply entrenched rivers, small bands of hunter-gatherers had once hooked catfish, suckers, and gar. Roaming the floodplains and uplands, they had speared and snared whatever game they could, from rabbits and snakes to rock squirrels and deer. And in the shady rock shelters, they had roasted the starchy bulbs of desert plants such as lechuguilla and sotol. Alert to any opportunity, they had missed little of economic value.

But they had more on their minds than the material world, says Turpin, pointing to a shadowy grotto in the east wall of the canyon. As the boat nudges up to the shoreline below Panther Cave, I spy the unmistakable lines of its namesake—the 9-foot-long cougar leaping along the back wall. Painted blood red and frozen forever in a lethal pounce, the giant cougar, or panther as it is known in local parlance, still blazes across the rocky canvas after thousands of years. "I think there's six different panther figures in there," says Turpin, stopping to admire the great cat from the shore. "But of course, he's the winner. He's King Kong."

Scrambling up the path, past Texas mountain laurel and thorn acacia, I follow Turpin as she darts through a small door in the wire fence that now protects the paintings from vandals. Under the tawny overhang of rock, we crane our necks as we stare up at the wild profusion of figures sprawling over more than 500 square feet of the wall. Black, rust red, orangy yellow, giant human forms loom high above our heads, following the sweeping curve of rock like living things. Painted one on top of another, they rise, collide, evaporate into their neighbors; the arm of one blends into the staff of another. Lighter than air, one small human figure levitates up the wall, his long hair standing literally on end. Nearby, a

The nine-foot-long figure of a panther that guards Panther Cave. (Courtesy of the author.)

grotesque crablike creature scuttles through the ether, while a herd of deer succumbs to hunters' spears.

Standing quietly back from the wall, her hands tucked in the pockets of her cotton pants, Turpin mulls over the dense thicket of figures. Like other murals painted in what has come to be known as the Pecos River style, this faded wall of color firmly resists snap interpretations. With its competing flocks of figures, its alien shapes and bizarre radiating lines, it overwhelms the eye. And as researchers have ascertained, there are no local oral traditions to help unlock the meaning: All native residents of the Lower Pecos had succumbed to disease and warfare by the end of the sixteenth century, long before researchers arrived in the region.

By poring over the figures carefully, however, Turpin and others have detected clear rules governing their portrayal. As she studies the wall, she explains that the giant elongated human figures always occupy the most prominent positions in the panels, their arms extended wide and their faces blank and featureless. Waving weapons such as spears and clubs, they dangle strange prickly ornaments from their arms and wrists. "You know that it's a pattern that has some meaning because it's so repetitive," says Turpin, "repetition being the mode of communication and ritual."

But what kind of ritual was it? During the late 1960s, Texas scholar William Newcomb theorized that the central human figures were shamans engaged in ritual dances of an ancient mescal-bean cult. Among historic tribes in the American south, shaman members of this cult consumed potent drinks made from the seeds of the Texas mountain laurel. Commonly known as mescal beans, the scarlet-colored seeds contained a poison that rendered the cultists unconscious; upon awakening, they told of powerful visions they had seen. Perhaps, suggested Newcomb, the panels depicted sacred dances of the mescal-bean shamans. The seeds seem to have been well known to the people of the Lower Pecos: Excavators unearthed dozens of samples in painted caves of the region.

Turpin, however, was unconvinced. In her surveying she often found Texas mountain laurel growing wild along the

At Panther Cave, one of many human figures portrayed with arms extended and weapons held in both hands. (Courtesy of the author.)

edges of Lower Pecos caves. So the brilliant scarlet seeds recovered by excavators could easily have been scattered along cave floors by agents of nature other than humans. But Turpin was intrigued by the suggestion that the large human figures were shamans. For years, researchers had suggested that shamanism arrived in North America with the first migrants, but little was known about its early practice on the continent. Could the painted panels of the Lower Pecos, with their thousands of figures, portray the mystical experiences of early shamans?

To test the idea, Turpin began immersing herself in the scientific literature on the religion and its complex system of beliefs. Among modern shamanistic cultures from Siberia to Chile, she discovered, people told of a time long ago when the earthly and spirit worlds were one. At some point in the past, however, the two realms sadly splintered apart, and humankind lost its ability to commune with gods and supernatural beings. Only a chosen few, the shamans, were now capable of crossing the great divide between the worlds: Their method of transport was the trance. Forsaking their earthbound bodies in an induced state of rapture, they called on the help of certain guardian animals and embarked on the perilous voyage to the otherworld. There they confronted deities and waged supernatural battles in order to see into the past, divine the future, cure illness, and escort the souls of the dead to their final home. "I like to call them supramen," says Turpin, "because they were over everything, by the very fact they could die and be reborn."

Had the Lower Pecos artists represented these beliefs in their art? Turpin began poring over the patterns of painted

A painting of one section of Panther Cave by early rock-art expert Forrest Kirkland. This section clearly depicts humans with spiny objects—possibly the fruit and other parts of the hallucinogenic Datura *plant, also known as thorn apple or devil's-apple. (By permission of the University of Texas Press.)*

figures for clues. Throughout the region, she noticed, only one form ever approached the human figures in size or prominence—the cougar. And as she studied the murals in Seminole Canyon, she saw a strange link between human and feline. At Panther Cave and elsewhere, Lower Pecos artists had endowed certain human figures with distinctive cougar attributes—claws, alert cat ears, and striped underbellies. Perhaps the artists were portraying shamans in the act of shape-shifting—assuming the protective form of a guardian animal for the dangerous passage to the otherworld. "This is the shaman who transforms into the largest and most power-ful animal here," says Turpin, pointing up at the tall, rust-red figure of the panther shaman.

Such beliefs, she adds, were common among shamanistic cultures. In Europe, for example, the ancient notion of shape-shifting gave birth to legends of werewolves; in Africa, it spawned tales of "were-crocodiles." Throughout most of Cen-tral and South America, however, it nurtured beliefs in "were-jaguars." Among the Campa of Peru, for example, people described the stealth of humanlike jaguars who prowled the forests at night in search of prey. In the Mexican highlands, people talked of similar creatures who stalked the darkness in feline form. And among certain Maya groups, these beliefs be-came so deeply engrained that the word *balam* served for both "jaguar" and "sorcerer."

As Turpin wandered the Lower Pecos, pondering over the strange panels, she began to decipher other figures, too. On some cave walls, she noticed small flocks of birds hovering be-side the shamans like avian guards of honor. On others, the metaphor of flight was extended, as humans assumed feath-ered wings and soared horizontally along rock-shelter ceilings. Entranced, Turpin recalled accounts of shamanic journeys to the sacred realm in which the mystics had described a birdlike flight of their souls. Among certain cultures in Siberia, ritual-ists frequently donned feathered robes in preparation for their difficult voyages.

Dodging hostile forces, often represented in the rock art by a rain of spears, the shamans described their entrance to the sacred realm through a small, circular portal. "See that hole over there?" asks Turpin, walking over to the back wall of Panther Cave and pointing at a large painted red dot. "See the circle with the lines coming out and the bird rising out of that? That's what I think is the hole of the universe, the portal to the divine." Recent psychological studies, moreover, suggest that such an image stems directly from human neural wiring. When entering deep, drug-induced trances, experimental subjects consistently report the sensation of being drawn down a vortex or through a deep hole.

Indeed, a belief in sacred portals may help explain why ancient artists chose these cave walls as their canvases. More than places of shelter, these dark grottoes may have become entrances to the spirit world. To illustrate the point, Turpin tells a story as we climb back into the boat and head back up the Rio Grande. Some years ago, she explains, she and a small team began excavations in a dark, bell-jar-shaped sinkhole near the rim of Seminole Canyon. Descending the narrow vertical shaft by ladder, the team reached a large subterranean chamber whose floor was littered with splinters of human bone. As the excavations proceeded, many of Turpin's colleagues concluded that the hole was used as a hasty dumping ground for the dead. "Everybody went, 'oh look, they just threw 'em away, they just threw 'em down the hole,'" she says.

But as Turpin studied the sinkhole, she began to see another possibility. With its vertical shaft belling into a large subterranean chamber, the sinkhole may have come to symbolize both an earthen birth canal and passage to the otherworld. Four thousand years ago and more, grieving relatives had carried their infant and elderly dead to the underground chamber, sliding them gently down the chute to return them to the darkened realm from which they came. "It was just a perfect symbolic rebirth," Turpin says finally, shaking her head at the memory. "It's that same old mythical portal to the earth."

✦ ✦ ✦

Tucking away pipe and tobacco, Jimmy Zintgraff leads the
way down the snaking path to the White Shaman site, alert to
the slightest sound. A small, wiry man in suspenders, neatly
pressed white shirt and canvas pants, the white-haired photographer looks more like a kindly pastor leading a church
picnic than a man packing a pistol. But Zintgraff is nothing if
not full of surprises. Grandson of a Texas Ranger, the courtly
San Antonio resident has come well prepared to blast the
trail's resident rattlesnake to kingdom come should it err by
putting in an appearance this afternoon.

Zintgraff, it transpires, doesn't take kindly to intruders in
these parts. Since finding and recording the White Shaman site
more than twenty-five years ago, he has taken up its protection
with true missionary zeal. Persuading a local philanthropist
to purchase the property for The Rock Art Foundation, a San
Antonio–based group dedicated to the preservation of the
paintings, he has succeeded admirably. As we reach the painted
overhang without so much as glimpsing a rattler (or Texas two-
stepper, as they are known here—"one step, two steps and

*A headless shaman shimmers along the main panel at the White
Shaman site. (Courtesy of the author.)*

you're dead," explains one of my companions), Zintgraff strides up with quiet reverence to the panels. In front of him, the White Shaman shimmers, headless and ascendant, against the golden-colored rock. Nearby, a huge painted larval monster wriggles up the back wall, while a flock of elongated humans waft in the cosmic breeze.

As I stand back staring, trying to take in its meaning, I wonder about the state of mind that conceived such unearthly images. Among some North American cultures, shamans regularly sought union with the spirit world by methods as diverse as dancing, fasting, and bloodletting. But here in the Lower Pecos they seem to have taken a more direct route. According to scholar Carolyn Boyd, the mystic artists of these canyons likely conceived many of their visions after consuming potent hallucinogenic plants. "I do think that what they are painting are experiences they had under the influence of these plants," says Boyd.

An artist, muralist, and archaeologist, Boyd began looking into the subject five years ago, while analyzing the Pecos River style of art and reading published studies of tribal groups in northern Mexico and the American Southwest. As she was sketching the mural at the White Shaman site one day, her attention was suddenly transfixed by the small, reddened figure of a human with deerlike antlers tipped by black dots. The image harkened back strongly to something she'd read. "I said wait a minute—the black dots on the antler tines, where have I heard about that before? Where have I heard about that?"

Turning it over in her mind, she remembered reading of an ancient divinity, part human and part deer, revered by the Huichol people of Mexico. Often called "the peyote tribe," the Huichol had long resisted Christianity, holding true to their shamanic traditions. Living on small ranches along the slopes of the Sierra Madre Occidental, the Huichol still spoke of an ancestral homeland in the Chihuahuan desert. Each fall, Huichol shamans led a pilgrimage there to collect a small, carrot-shaped cactus: the powerful hallucinogen peyote. According to tribal tradition, peyote was a sacred plant first carried to earth on the tines of a deer-god. To honor this divinity, pilgrims fastened some of the cacti to deer antlers carried along on the quest.

Had the people of the Lower Pecos subscribed to similar beliefs nearly 4,200 years ago? Certainly the artists painted antlered human forms repeatedly on their rock-shelter walls. And archaeological evidence suggested they knew peyote well. While excavating a series of high, painted caves overlooking the Rio Grande, researchers from the Witte Museum unearthed paraphernalia similar to that employed in modern peyote rituals. More intriguing still, they also found scatterings of peyote, which grows only in isolated spots in the region, along the sandy floors. When radiocarbon-dated recently, two of these specimens proved to be 7,000 years old—the oldest known peyote in the world.

"I said, okay, that's interesting, but it's still not enough proof," recalls Boyd. Digging further into published accounts of today's peyote pilgrimage, she began turning up a remarkable series of parallels to the images recorded at the White Shaman site. To symbolize a spirit of unity before they set out, for example, Huichol shamans instruct the pilgrims to grasp part of a long cactus-fiber cord; the cord is then scorched by fire. With ritual purification complete, the pilgrims then depart from their village in single file, each carrying a lighted candle. Stopping at last, they face the east, holding up candles to the ascending sun. On the White Shaman mural, five large, equally spaced humans hold fiery torches in both hands; each is linked by a serpentine white cord darkened at one end. "It was just incredible," says Boyd, "because it was one thing after another that started revealing itself."

In considering the evidence, she now suggests that specific physiological effects of peyote may have profoundly shaped both religious belief and art. Those consuming peyote, she notes, are often seized by an initial sense of physical and mental exhilaration. Among some native cultures in Mexico, runners eat peyote to whet their speed and boost their endurance during footraces. On occasion, witnesses of some modern rites have described participants "jumping like deer" after swallowing the plant. Such athleticism on the part of an ancient shaman, suggests Boyd, could have inspired belief in a divinity half deer, half human. "So I think you have your sacred deer people, the people who followed the peyote shaman."

As intoxication from the plant deepens, moreover, subjects report their first swirling hallucinations. Laced with mescaline, the plant triggers visions both nightmarish and beautiful, and fosters a strong sense of disembodiment. "No part of my body was subject to the laws of gravitation," reported one experimental subject—a German physician—in the 1920s. "Extremely fantastic figures appeared before my eyes. I was very excited, perspired and shivered, and was kept in a state of ceaseless wonder" (Anderson 1980). Among the mystics of the Lower Pecos, such powerful visions were likely painted hours or days after their trances ended, when eye-hand coordination returned.

In Boyd's view, the peyote murals of the region now stand as the world's oldest known record of hallucinogen-inspired altered states. "It's the first evidence we have visually, it's in the sediments and pulled together through ethnography, to say yes, 4,000 years ago, people were using hallucinogenic plants," she notes. But as her research proceeds, she is rapidly amassing evidence of other equally potent plants. "I think we're going to find a great many more through the rock art—not just hallucinogens, but medicinal plants that were very much a part of ritual."

One of the most intriguing lines of evidence relates to the spiny ovals that protrude from the painted staffs held by most human figures. (See the illustration on page 59.) For years, researchers have mused over their significance, suggesting that they could be medicine bags or pouches fashioned from hollowed prickly pear pads. But Boyd sees matters differently. The spiny objects, she notes, bear a startling resemblance to the calyx, stem, and thorn-covered fruit of *Datura*, commonly known as thorn apple or devil's-apple. And archaeological evidence supports her contention: In the late 1970s botanist Philip Dering identified several seeds of the plant along the 4,700-year-old floor of a Lower Pecos rock shelter.

Bearing fruit and fiber spiked with potent chemicals, the genus *Datura* acts powerfully on the human nervous system, producing symptoms ranging from vivid hallucinations and deep sleep to temporary paralysis of the lower limbs. In the Old World, datura was long associated with witchcraft; in the western hemisphere, it has been prized by shamans. Among the Zuni, for example, rain priests dust their own eyes and ears with small amounts of the powdered root to foster communication with avian spirits at night; among the Tubatulabal of California, ritualists prepare special datura drinks for adolescents undergoing sacred puberty rites.

But among the Huichol, where the old peyote cult flourishes, datura is greatly feared as a dangerous plant; only the peyote shaman can handle it with impunity. Perplexed by such views, Boyd began searching for some explanation. In her reading, she came across a Huichol story of an evil being who once ruled over all sorcerers on earth; the spirit's name was Datura Person. Jealous of his great rival, the deer-god, Datura Person once tried to tempt the Huichol away from peyote with his strong potions. But it was no use. Armed with peyote, the sacred Deer Person resoundingly vanquished the sorcerer, restoring peace to the world once again.

Could such traditions record the ancient rivalry between two powerful shamans in the Chihuahuan desert thousands of years ago? It is still far from clear, but Boyd now believes that the rich rock art of the Lower Pecos, with its tantalizing throngs of figures, brims with clues to these and other mysteries. Painted long before the invention of paper in the New World, these enigmatic panels resemble the later hand-painted codices of Mesoamerica, recording tribal mythology, sacred ritual, and spiritual vision. For Boyd and others, the challenge now is to decode them with the help of ethnography. "What we have is uniquely accessible facts of history that tell of their own creation," she says, a tone of wonder in her voice. "They are there and we are now finally starting to be able to read them."

✦   ✦   ✦

In the silence of the morning, I pick my way down the rubble-littered wall of Rattlesnake Canyon, trying not to think about the heat. Above, in a flawless pewter sky, the sun has already developed a hard, steely gleam; the air hardly moves. "It's the worst kind of sky," says Zintgraff, mopping his forehead as he rests at the side of the trail. Sweat trickles down my back. In the canyon below, Turpin and two others disappear into a towering thicket of desert willow, crashing against trunks and snapping slender branches. I follow, welcoming the shade. Along the muddy ground, javelina skulls whiten in the cool quiet.

Rising 20 feet or so in the air, the willows wall out the world, reducing our vision to a green tunnel. Emerging at last, I straighten and stare in wonder. Along the canyon floor lie small pools of clear green water, like something from a classical Chinese garden. High along the rim, slender canes of ocotillo, each tipped with a brilliant crimson bloom, bend in greeting. Below, on scattered ledges, prickly pear cactuses cascade like giant green water drops, while claret-cup cactuses brim with ruby flowers. "They're like little hanging gardens," says Turpin, gazing up at them with a smile.

Turning, she leads the way to a shady, painted wall, and as I stand before scenes of soaring humans, aloft in rapture, I feel a sudden, unexpected kinship to these ancient artists. Wrapped in thought and wonder, they once walked this narrow canyon, reveling in its secret harmonies of water and shade. Alive to its beauty, they returned here time and again, choosing this rugged wall for their unearthly visions. Standing quietly, humbled by the grandeur of the human imagination, I glimpse the wonders of their calling.

For thousands of years, shamans in these parts sought communion with the mysterious otherworld. Consuming plants endowed with secret powers, they divined the unfoldings of the future and bid farewell to the dead. In years to come, scholars will undoubtedly unearth earlier evidence of such divine plants, for shamanistic cultures, by their very nature, were vision seekers. For many thousands of years, people searched for doorways to the divine; in all likelihood, such beliefs accompanied them when they first migrated from the tundras of Siberia.

In the shady cool of the morning, I am reluctant to leave this corner of paradise. Caught in the same spell, Turpin leads us to a small alcove farther up the canyon. Along a broad shelf of white rock, we stretch out in silence along the cool rock, staring up at the sky. In the far distance, a canyon wren sings, its sweetness echoing along the towering walls. Turpin looks over and smiles. "Maybe this is what they mean by the unbearable lightness of being."

4

THE NOUVEAUX RICHES

Keatley Creek, British Columbia

It's the same the world over
It's the poor what gets the blame
It's the rich what gets the pleasure
Isn't it a bloody shame.

—ANON

In the fading light, wind teases at the trees, rustling dry branches like rattles as we rouse the dead. There are six of us tonight—archaeologists, fishers, and one writer—hunched in heavy sweaters and parkas around a campfire in an ancient winter village above the Fraser River. Beyond the clearing where we sit, willows and ghostly white cottonwoods stripe the banks of the nearby creek, concealing ruins of long-abandoned sweat lodges. Along the narrow footpath behind us, a forest of twisted sagebrush rises up the slope, cloaking remains of charred roofs and fallen gables. Pale roots curl around the crumbling skeletons of village dogs. Tonight, all is silent, all is returning to nature. In the mountains above, only black bears stir in their sleep, catching the first faint scent of spring.

Still, we are not alone. Perhaps the dead hear our laughter. In the flickering firelight, we play lehal, the bone game favored in this canyon for hundreds, maybe thousands, of years. Lacking a set of bones, archaeologist Brian Hayden has whittled branches into thumb-sized playing pieces. They have yet to bring us luck. In the shadowy light, Hayden picks up another counter and tosses it over to Desmond Peters Sr., a stocky, barrel-shaped man in blue baseball cap and well-worn plaid shirt. Former chief of the Pavilion Band just down the road, Peters catches it neatly with one hand and arranges it on his growing pile. "One time when people played this game," he says, his dark brown eyes gleaming, "they bet their tents, their rifles, their wives, everything. In Victoria, in the longhouse there, I won $3,000."

Tonight, however, he settles for a friendlier game. Divided into two teams, we stare at each other across the fire. The object is to guess which opponent, which hand, finally conceals the marked bone. It is no easy matter. Gripping the whittled pieces in his fist, Peters fixes us with the gaze of a snake charmer. As Hayden strikes up the obligatory song, the former chief nods, then begins weaving his arms through the air. With strange hypnotic grace, he slips his hands down the arms of first one teammate, then another. All sinuous movement, his fingers dart and feint, slithering restlessly across open palms. Hayden finishes his song. Studying his opponents intently, the scientist points to the young man on the left, convinced Peters has palmed off the notched bone. But the scientist is no match for the conjurer's art. With a broad smile, the old man slowly uncurls the fingers of his right hand: Inside lies the contentious bone.

For Hayden, an authority on prehistoric life along this stretch of the Fraser, this is more than a casual evening's sport: It is yet another sortie into the strange and tantalizing past of the Keatley Creek site. For nearly a decade now, he and his students have been journeying to this remote village. Perched along the edge of the Northwestern Plateau in Canada, some 150 miles northeast of Vancouver, Keatley Creek is only now divulging its secrets. Bordering the Fraser River, once one of the world's greatest salmon spawning grounds, it long reveled in abundance. In its circular earthen houses, nearly 1,500 residents passed the cold winter nights in feasting, ceremony and sleep. And they were not alone. Nearby, along a twenty-mile stretch of the Fraser, researchers have mapped seven other similar villages. "Even if only half of these sites are contemporaneous," says Hayden, "it's an enormous population for this area."

By such measures, Keatley Creek clearly commands attention. But numbers are only a small part of its attraction. While carefully exhuming the village houses and combing forgotten ethnographies, Hayden and his colleagues uncovered a complex society of traders, administrators, slave owners, and luxury-lovers. Counting their wealth in vast stores of dried salmon and salmon oil, the people of Keatley Creek once traded for the finest of everything in the Pacific Northwest— jade, copper, furs, slaves. Dominated by elegant nobles fond of politicking and the pleasures of the hunt, and shouldered by a class of working poor, the ancient village remained a powerhouse along the Northwestern Plateau for hundreds of years, until its mysterious collapse around A.D. 850.

Fascinated by these discoveries, Hayden and his colleagues are now examining the very foundations of village life. How, they now wonder, did such wealth and poverty first arise along the Fraser more than 2,500 years ago? How did nobles there manage to acquire the finest foods, robes, and properties while others fell into indigency, too poorly dressed to journey outside the village in winter? What separated the rich from the poor? And what ultimately happened to the once-populous village? Could it have fallen victim to a violent natural disaster?

"To me, the interesting thing is to find out what was happening here," explains Hayden on an early April morning at his camp along the creek. Leaning against a wooden table bearing the name of Amnesty International and littered with candle-topped wine bottles, homemade tin lanterns, and an assortment of health-food magazines, he smiles reflectively, tightening the lid on a jar of honey. Along the creek behind, a woodpecker taps out its insistent rhythm. Jays squabble in the nearby trees. Paying them little mind, Hayden dumps his breakfast dishes in the washbasin, stopping for a moment to run a finger along his scalp in search of suspected wood ticks. "You don't want to let them live," he explains absently, coming up empty-handed. "They're sure to come back and haunt you."

Tall and athletic, with intense blue eyes, silver beard, and a barely tamed mass of graying hair, Hayden is not always an easy person to warm to. Wrapped in a world of abstraction and theory, he finds small talk difficult, modern social conventions boring. But at age fifty, he still relishes the rough-and-tumble of fieldwork. With friend and former student Susan Wilson, a quirky, outgoing woman in her early thirties, he has spent the past week at Keatley Creek, stripping off shubbery and laying out trenches in a small pit house. Ready to begin excavations in earnest, Hayden is anxious to be off. Reaching for his pack and water thermos, he hustles out of camp and leads the way up the hill past the overgrown volleyball court and the two-seated outhouse known affectionately as the Lew—or alternatively as the Binford—after renowned American archaeologist Lewis Binford.

True to his own lights, Hayden has never favored the beaten path. Born in New Jersey, the son of an advertising executive, he has long displayed a talent for meticulous research. As a young graduate student fascinated with stone tools, he spent a year wandering the sweltering western desert of Australia, watching white-haired aboriginal elders work flint into choppers and scrapers. As an expert on Iroquoian cultures, he launched an ambitious study of a massive—and largely undisturbed—village site slated to become an international airport. But he soon found himself mired in controversy. Stubbornly refusing to speed up work in such an important site with road graders, the young researcher reluctantly packed it in. Deeply disappointed, he accepted a teaching job at Simon Fraser University in British Columbia. There he began casting around for a new focus for his research.

Far from developers and perfectly suited for research into past societies, Keatley Creek filled the bill: Hayden was entranced. And as I follow him up the ridge this morning, hurrying a little to keep pace, I can understand his passion for this place. To the west, the massive Camelsfoot Mountains loom steep and gray from forests of dark green, girded only by a slender mountain road. Beyond, high frozen peaks stretch like white spires to the far horizon. On the slopes below us, deer trails slant skittishly across faded green terraces, while mountain streams course clear and cool down willowy ravines. Out of sight, tucked inside the steep inner canyon, the Fraser River rushes southward, hurrying on to the Pacific.

It was down this river, explains Hayden, that the first party of white and Métis fur traders, led by burly, red-haired Simon Fraser, paddled in 1808. A partner in the Northwest Company, Fraser had struck out westward in search of supply and travel routes to the Pacific. Some ten miles downstream from Keatley Creek, he and his companions stumbled upon a well-

The steep inner canyon of the Fraser River. (Courtesy of the author.)

provisioned camp of salmon hunters. Dressed in bark capes, shell necklaces, and salmon-skin shoes, they welcomed the hungry travelers, offering them baskets brimming with berries, wild vegetables, dog meat, and salmon. "The Chief made a great harangue," confided Fraser later in his journal, "& then invited us to his *shade*, where we were treated with great hospitality" (Fraser 1960). So content were some of Fraser's men that they soon contemplated going native, remaining with their hosts rather than returning east with their employer.

And such prosperity shaped life here for hundreds, likely thousands, of years. As Hayden reaches the top of the ridge, he follows the path, slowing beside the rim of a great bowl-shaped hollow. Carpeted in high sagebrush, the circular rim marks the place where earthen walls once rose to a sod and timber roof. Looking up, I gaze across the basin. For hundreds of feet in all directions, similar craters pock the broad terrace—some small as huts, others large as modern suburban houses, most no more than a few feet apart. "They go just about up to the tree line there and all the way down to the far end of that terrace," nods Hayden. "That would be about eight to ten acres, the core of this site."

It was such urban sprawl, in fact, that first aroused his interest. With more than 115 buildings crammed side by side, Keatley Creek clearly dwarfed earlier encampments of hunter-gatherers in the region. And as Hayden tramped up and down the steep slopes, gazing at the deep hollows, he was fascinated by their widely varying sizes. Detailed research by others in the region suggested that both large and small structures alike were residences. But why did some people pass the coldest months of the year in tiny huts, while others flocked together under one large roof?

Early accounts of the Upper Lillooet held a few tantalizing clues. A local native group who wintered in pit houses along this stretch of the Fraser River, the Upper Lillooet were clearly closely related to prehistoric populations in the area. And according to turn-of-the-century ethnographer James Teit, they had once known a striking class system. At the top of Upper Lillooet society were clan chiefs so lofty that others

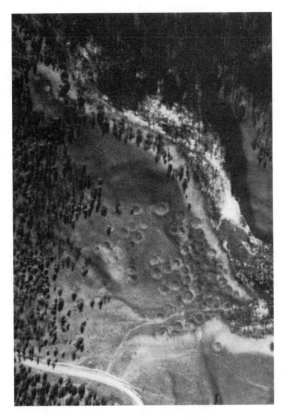

Circular house pits crowd the rolling hillside near Keatley Creek. (Courtesy of Brian Hayden.)

feared to speak to them directly. Surrounded by wives and retainers, hunting dogs and pet falcons, these chiefs were dressed in the finest painted buckskin and wrapped in the warmest furs. At the bottom of Lillooet society were slaves so abject that some were sacrificed to serve their masters in the next world.

Had the smallest houses at Keatley Creek belonged to such slaves? And had the roomiest houses, five in all, belonged to chiefly families and their retainers? To test the theory, Hayden selected a disparate sample of residences that dated to the final years of the village, around A.D. 850. Hacking down sagebrush and peeling back layers of roots and pebbly dirt, burnt bark and charcoal, crew members set to work searching for strata containing the house floors. "If you want to get at social differences and organization," explains Hayden, "you really have to look at living floors and see what kinds of families were living in there, what kinds of activities were going on."

As the work proceeded, team members soon marveled at the extremes of village life. In one small dwelling, measuring just over 400 square feet, three families had crowded together in the cold and dark. Lighting few fires and leaving no trace of the tools needed to make buckskin shirts and leggings, they had braved the bitter winter temperatures in only thin bark clothing, too poorly dressed to venture outside long enough to gather firewood. Such misery, however, was relatively rare. In medium-sized homes, which sheltered nearly 70 percent of the population, residents had relished more frequent fires, filling meals, and some leather clothing, and had acquired a few luxuries such as copper. "I'd see them as middle-class people," says Hayden.

In the largest house, however, it was a different story. Spreading out across the cavernous pit, crew members were soon surrounded by tokens of wealth and privilege—the stone carving of a serpent's head, smooth white seashells for making necklaces, soapstone pipes for smoking tobacco, quartzite scrapers for fashioning deerskin clothing, pieces of polished jade likely worked by slaves. And there had been no shortage of food. Dense scatterings of salmon and deer bones littered the floor, while skeletal remains of dogs lined storage pits. Descended not from wolves but from coyotes, these hounds had served their masters well—as draft animals, hunting dogs, ritual sacrifices, and even delicacies for favored guests. "I think they were real status items," says Hayden with a nod.

Such luxuries seemed to spell the good life for families in the large house, but the researcher was determined to take a closer look. Back on campus, team members set to work analyzing the spatial distribution of everything from cooking stones to tool-making debris. Hayden was soon fascinated. While eight families had once wiled away the coldest days of winter in the house, they had enjoyed widely varying standards of living. Along one half of the house, individuals had reclined beside generous fires and dined on meals from spacious storage pits. Along the other side, they had shivered in the cold and consumed a spartan fare. Differences in class could hardly be clearer. A thousand years ago and more, Hayden now suggests, wealthy, well-dressed nobles had lived elbow to elbow with the commoners and slaves who assisted and served them.

But one sector of this huge house continued to puzzle the researcher. Along the southern zone, excavators unearthed few stone tools, fewer animal or fish bones. It looked empty, but this seeming abandonment made little sense. Facing the winter sun, the spot would have been the most coveted in the house. As Hayden mulled over the problem, he remembered that the choicest cuts of meat seldom contain any bones at all, and that among west coast tribes such as the Nuu-chal-nulth, the most important individuals generally devoted their time to politicking and administering—activities that required no stone tools. After considering the matter carefully, Hayden now suggests that this zone was reserved for those with the greatest power and wealth of all—the family of the administrative or house chief.

✦ ✦ ✦

With a cool spring wind at our backs, we stand along the edge of a mountain road, frozen in time as we peer down at the restless waters of the Fraser. Frothing white, almost lathering with the sheer effort of its passage through a channel only 100 feet wide, the muddy river twists and turns through the narrow canyon below. Swirling in giant eddies, sweeping up black gravel from the channel, it rolls over rapids and pours past ancient fishing rocks with names like *sxetl'* ("drop-off"), *xwusesús* ("foaming") and *púlhmekw* ("boiling on bottom"). On the water-slicked banks above, gray drying racks catch the light like skeletons.

That anything could survive these rapids, much less defeat them, seems unbelievable. But in the white water below us swims the season's first run of salmon. Journeying home after years of fattening in the cool dark waters of the ocean, schools of chinook muscle their way upstream to the spawning grounds. Battered by rocks, buffeted by currents, they hurl onward, driven by ancient instinct and an almost supernatural strength. Over the next six months, thousands of sockeye and chinook will follow, hurtling over these rocky stretches of river. It is a sight not soon forgotten. And before commercial fishing battered the Fraser River stocks in the mid-1990s, eight million fish or more tested their mettle here at Six Mile Rapids, literally darkening the water with their fins.

Such prolificacy, such fleeting plenitude, has never been lost on those who dwelled in this canyon. In years past, Upper Lillooet families from Pavilion and other nearby reservation towns clambered down the steep trails to the rapids here, as their forefathers had for generations. Standing on the slippery banks, setting store-bought gill nets or homemade hoop nets into the swirling waters, men began the exhausting and often dangerous work of hauling in a year's supply of salmon. Even the very strongest tired quickly. "Most people go fishing to relax," says Hayden, shaking his head beside me. "But not around here. When you go fishing, you take your life in your hands."

In all likelihood, he explains, the ancient residents of Keatley Creek fished in much the same way. Taking up residence in large fish camps along Six Mile Rapids in late July, men, women, and children waited patiently for the largest runs. Rising at first light, the men gathered together their gear and set off down the slopes to the fishing rocks. In the cool of the morning, they swung their long-handled nets into the quiet back eddies. At the height of season, sockeye concentrated here, marshaling their strength for the rapids; nets were soon filled. As the men swiftly dispatched the wriggling haul, young boys waited to pack them up the hill.

In camp, women laid out the first catch of the morning. With deft hands, they began splitting the fish along the backbone, scoring the brilliant red flesh with deep cuts of their knives. By the end of a good day, nearly 100 sockeye might flutter from a family's wooden racks; by the end of a good year, salmon might spill from their caches, leaving more than enough for traders from the coast and the interior. Arriving daily with their wares—shell beads, soapstone pipes, bird feathers, pieces of jade, warm furs, and slaves taken in recent raids—traders bartered eagerly for the camp's produce. Dried salmon from this region, after all, was renowned. Along the arid gorge, wind dried the fish swiftly, preventing rot or maggots that often ruined coastal catches. And chinook and sockeye caught here tasted richer and moister than any netted farther upstream, for they still retained natural fat and oil.

As the runs thinned and frost silvered the sagebrush, old men in the camps began gathering the discarded fish heads and fins for an even greater delicacy. Boiling these scraps in stone basins, they carefully ladled out the reddish brown oil, storing it in fine bottles of salmon skin. Brimming with the calories that hunter-gatherers often found hard to come by, these delicate bottles were coveted by native bands across the Northwestern Plateau. "If you want to stay warm in the wintertime, you need a lot of food that's going to produce calories," says Hayden. "That's why salmon oil and fat was so valuable and that's why people used to pile it on their food. The tales and myths that ethnographer James Teit recorded are full of references to eating and storing fat."

To catch the fish richest in oil—the chinook—fishers went to extraordinary lengths. Unlike smaller and weaker members of its family, chinook shunned river edges, favoring deeper and faster waters. Only in a few well-known spots along the Middle Fraser Canyon did strong currents force the fish close to shore-bound outcrops. There, some men built elaborate scaffolds and platforms of poles and ropes. Edging out along their length, they lowered huge bag nets measuring 6 feet wide into the water. As the river raged below them, some must have wondered what the waters would offer up. The largest chinook, reaching 70 pounds in weight, hit the nets like cannonballs: The strike of a school could prove disasterous. "They're fighters, you know," says Desmond Peters Sr. "And they're traveling fast when they hit the nets." In the shock of the moment, men were sometimes knocked off their feet. Those who had refused to anchor themselves to shore with a lifeline were almost certainly doomed. Tumbling into the furious water, they struggled for air and were swept downstream, hammering against the rocks.

✦   ✦   ✦

Silent with concentration, Hayden bends over the grass-edged trench, knees angling through ancient ripped jeans. It is mid-morning at Keatley Creek: The sun washes down in a warm light. On the slope above, Wilson heaves another heavy bucket of dirt and pebbles into the screen, her enthusiasm for the work clearly waning. But Hayden pays little mind. Along the floor of the trench, rows of tiny translucent salmon ribs, slender as needles, bristle from the earth. Hayden picks up one and bends it softly between thumb and forefinger, testing its elasticity. "It's almost as though they were for someone's dinner a week or so ago," he says finally, sliding it unbroken into a plastic bag.

Beyond any doubt, the residents of Keatley Creek consumed vast quantities of salmon. In fact, studies of human skeletal remains from the region show that people here ate few other staples. Extracting small quantities of a protein known as collagen from the bones, researcher Brian Chisholm and his associates measured the ratios of certain key carbon isotopes in the substance. These ratios were then compared to those produced by other major foods. Some 5,000 years ago, they concluded, salmon made up nearly 40 percent of the human diet in this region; 3,000 years later, however, when Keatley Creek was booming, it had soared to a whopping 70 percent. Salmon had become the staff of life.

But what fascinated Hayden was the social revolution that had accompanied this dietary shift. As salmon became paramount on the Northwestern Plateau, taking over local economies and largely replacing most other types of food, families veered away from ancient traditions of charity and generosity. In villages such as Keatley Creek, people no longer shared food liberally with others in the community. And over

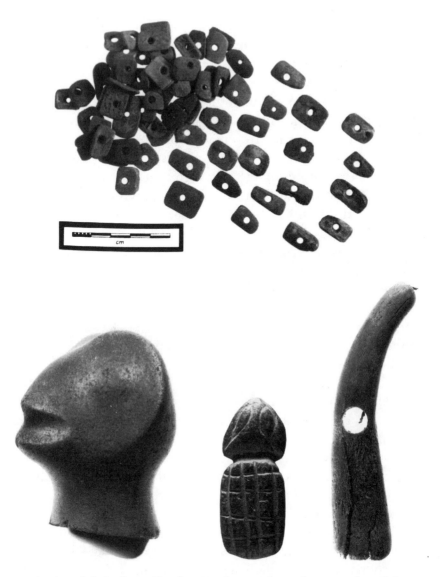

Intriguing debris from Keatley Creek: top, bone buttons found in a storage pit; bottom left, stone top of a woodworking tool shaped like an animal head; bottom middle, a snakelike sculpture made of serpentine; bottom right, a digging stick made of antler. (Photos by Phil Hobler; courtesy of Brian Hayden.)

time, a new social order of chiefs, nobles, commoners, and slaves emerged. Mulling over these radical departures from the past, Hayden wondered how they came about. How did a powerful class system arise?

It seemed an intractable problem, but while poring over fish bones from the village, student Kevin Berry came across a telling clue. Intrigued by a new technique for distinguishing the species of certain salmon bones, Berry was counting telltale growth rings along the tiny vertebrae, identifying ages of the individual fish at the time of their spawning runs. And as he sifted through the results, he could see that wealth had been intimately linked to particular types of salmon. In the poorest homes, for example, residents ate only pink salmon, a small and relatively flavorless species that could be easily landed from simple brush jetties along the riverbanks. More affluent homes, however, stocked more varied fare. In the largest residences, inhabitants dined on pink, sockeye, and chinook salmon. Indeed chinook made up nearly 35 percent of the meals.

Clearly, rich and poor had fished the river very differently. While paupers landed their catch along brush jetties, people of wealth and substance harvested theirs from fishing rocks. And this ancient pattern persisted into historic times. According to Upper Lillooet elders, certain families once owned the best fishing rocks in the region, some fifty or so spots in all. As prized as fertile fields were by the French peasantry, these rocks were faithfully passed down through the generations from father to son. In all likelihood, says Hayden now, families had once counted their wealth in river rocks. Those who controlled the best filled their storage pits and rafters with dried fish; those who cast their nets elsewhere learned to live with much less.

Perhaps, suggests Hayden, hunter-gatherers in the region first accepted such inequality because of the relative security afforded by fishing. Possessed of sturdy nets and reliable preservation methods, all families could set aside enough dried salmon in a good year to last them through the winter; no one worried unduly about starvation. "If you develop enough surplus so that everyone feels more or less comfortable," says Hayden, "then if someone wants to go ahead and develop a new fishing site by building a new platform and then use all of the produce from that for their own household, that's fine. They can go ahead and do that."

The trouble was that some families soon pushed for more. While analyzing stone tools and lithic debris unearthed in the village, Hayden and colleagues Ed Bakewell, Ted Danner, and Rob Gargett discovered that the largest houses had virtually monopolized certain valuable stone quarries. While the residents of house-pit five, for example, favored a fine-grained quartz known as chalcedony, those in number seven relied extensively on a distinctive speckled chert. "These people had privileged access, by one means or another, to the sources of this stone," says Hayden, sitting back on his heels. "And all these sources are up in the mountains."

In all likelihood, members of the large houses stocked up on this stone while traveling together to certain mountain valleys. A century or so ago, Upper Lillooet families journeyed to specific valleys each fall in order to hunt deer along privately owned fences. Constructed of poles and tree limbs and strung with bark-string snares, these fences were lethal traps for mule deer, one of the few local big-game species. While Hayden has yet to find any trace of such prehistoric fences in the region, he believes that wealthy families from Keatley Creek controlled similar hunting preserves and collected their stone while journeying to them. "It may well have something to do with that," he says.

And what impresses the cautious archaeologist most is the enduring nature of these rights. From the very bottoms of the house rims to the tops of the floors—an archaeological record spanning at least 1,400 years—residents consistently sharpened tools from exactly the same types of stone. From one generation to the next, they passed down ownership of key hunting and fishing reserves. To the astonished researcher, it now suggests that the great pit houses at Keatley Creek were far more than casual dwellings: They were residences of groups similar to the great clans of the historic Lil-

A man fishing for salmon using a traditional-style platform in the Lillooet area. (Courtesy of the Vancouver Public Library.)

looet culture. Living together under one roof, sharing in the labor, these families reaped the rewards of ancestral rights vested in their chief. "These house sites and the houses and everything else that went with them were owned and passed down from one generation to another for thousands of years," says Hayden with a smile. "No one ever dreamed that such enduring social groups were possible. They are like small corporations that lasted over 1,000 years."

✦   ✦   ✦

On the coldest nights of winter, when thick snow blanketed the mountains, the clans of this canyon once gave witness to their greatness. Inviting rivals to their smoky pit houses, members of the Bear, Coyote, and Frog clans donned their richest buckskin and set out heaping platters of deer meat, fat, and other delicacies. Around blazing fires, they handed out gifts of mountain-goat-wool blankets to their guests and watched as masked dancers reenacted the ancestral beginnings of their clan. "Some of these potlatches were great affairs," observed James Teit, "and clans tried to outdo one another by the quantity and value of their presents, thus showing to all the country that they were the most powerful, wealthy, and energetic" (Teit 1906).

For years now, Hayden has wondered whether such spectacles were ever held in the five largest houses at Keatley Creek. Like the Bear, Coyote, and Frog clans, the noble families of these houses would have vied strenuously with each other for the plums they all desired—rich trading partners, strong military allies, wealthy spouses, and the awed respect of commoners. And on the cold winter evenings, sequestered in their pit houses, residents would have had long hours to prepare for such pomp and ceremony. Intrigued by the possibility, Hayden set to work scouring the village for evidence.

Just outside the largest of the house pits, team members soon uncovered a huge roasting pit scattered with charred deer bone—a type of food rarely found in most village homes. On the high terrace above and along the creek bed below, crew members excavated two more food-preparation areas—suitable for large ceremonies. And as experts analyzed faunal remains excavated from some of the houses, they soon detected other evidence: deer antlers shaped to fit a headdress, and bear paws and raptor bones often worn by historic dancers when performing clan dances.

While Hayden continues to scour for more evidence, he now believes that elaborate feasts played a prominent part in village life here. And such celebrations, he suggests, must have been grand affairs. Attired in their finest clothes—glimmering necklaces of imported shell and rolled copper, soft buckskin shirts, and breeches trimmed with brilliant feathers—the hosts looked like billboards of the good life, as difficult to resist 1000 years ago as the pitches of Madison Avenue are today. "There was a lot of advertising going on," says Hayden. "They were saying, 'Come join us—there's lots of fringe benefits, lots of major benefits too.' "

And in all likelihood, these lavish events paid off handsomely on occasion. Among comparable societies on the Northwest Coast and New Guinea, for example, hosts often staged feasts for financial gain. When Kwakiutl families on the British Columbian coast invited rival groups to their potlatches, they expected them to reciprocate the extravagant gifts of fish oil and button blankets—with interest. "It's not a de facto obligation," Hayden notes, "but there's usually an attempt to pay back more than what is involved." Such investments made sound economic sense. In a good year, a wise chief could give away huge quantities of food—which would otherwise rot—in a costly feast. In poor years, when the salmon runs were sparser, he could call in the debts from his guests.

But the chiefs of Keatley Creek had to be sophisticated administrators to throw such feasts. Responsible for the prosperity of the entire house, they had to skillfully appraise the value of their investments and the financial worth of others. "They would have had to maintain some form of accounting system," says Hayden. "They would have had to know how much surplus was available, how it could be used, where it could be invested, what could be loaned out, what kinds of loans were outstanding. And that would have been a very central part of life among some of these groups here."

✦   ✦   ✦

In the flickering light, Hayden and I gather up plates and toss wishbones into the fire. Lantern in hand, Wilson sweeps up the pots and leads the way slowly down the hill, talking loudly. Carrying plates still steeped in the smell of barbequed chicken, the veteran hiker and former tree planter is worried about bears tonight. So now am I. Stepping over tree roots, bending back branches, I am alert to the slightest sound. But nothing stirs. Keatley Creek remains as still now as it was a thousand years ago, when the last inhabitants packed their things and set off down the slopes.

Abandoned to nature, the village conceals its final days well. After years of work, Hayden and his crews have unearthed no traces of violence or warfare, no signs of devastating disease. Anthropologists have recorded no tales or traces of the village in oral history, other than its name. For years, team members had little idea about the fate of the 1,500 residents here. What added to the puzzle, moreover, was the similarity between Keatley Creek and two other neighboring winter villages. All three had been deserted about the same time—around A.D. 850.

For Hayden, it seemed an intractable mystery until he came across the research of two local geographers. While studying sediments underlying river terraces near the town of Lillooet, several miles south of Keatley Creek, June Ryder and Michael Church stumbled across a strange anomaly. Amid the expected layers of channel gravel overlain by silts and sands from flooding, Ryder and Church discovered an unusual bed of coarse gravel covered by finer gravels, sediments, and windblown silt. To trained eyes, this layer clearly recorded an ancient catastrophe. At some point in the past, they reasoned, landslides downstream had thundered down across the bed of the river. Hemmed behind this natural dam, the Fraser River had flooded dramatically, forming a huge temporary lake here.

But when? While examining a road cut in the region, Ryder and Church noticed the outlines of a native storage pit at the base of the telltale flood layers. Luck was with them. In addition to fine sand, fragments of fish bone, and fire-cracked rock, the pit contained several small pieces of charcoal. When dispatched for radiocarbon dating, the charcoal proved to be some 1,180 years old. For Hayden, all the pieces suddenly started falling into place. "The widespread abandonment of the three major sites [is] almost contemporaneous with what appears to be a major rise in the river level, a major rise."

Just where the landslide pounded down into the Fraser may never be known with certainty. But the likeliest possibility can be seen today from a cliff south of Lillooet, where Texas Creek pours into the Fraser River. Angling down sharply to the river below, the rocky escarpment here is the legacy of two massive slides. Although Ryder has yet to obtain radiocarbon dates for either, she estimates, based on rates of river downcutting, that the first of these catastrophic slides occurred sometime within the past 5,000 years, the second within the last 2,000 years.

Intrigued, some researchers now wonder if a series of major earthquakes could have fractured these cliffs, triggering two landslides. Along the west coast of Washington and British Columbia, geophysicists have begun amassing evidence of an ancient cycle of mega-earthquakes capable of great destruction. But as Hayden cautions, considerably more evidence must be gathered before any conclusions can be reached. "It's one of those interesting ideas that you'd want lots more data to substantiate."

There is little doubt, however, that a major rockslide would have decimated salmon runs upriver. When a similar disaster struck along the Fraser River in 1913, notes Hayden, the returning fish were simply unable to hurtle over the rubble in their path. Stocks were nearly wiped out. Pink salmon runs, for example, immediately crashed from 38 million fish to insignificant numbers: Only with the construction of fish ladders along the Fraser in the late 1940s did they begin to rebound. Even so, recovery was painfully slow. Indeed, the runs failed to reach historic levels even by 1980 when the International Pacific Salmon Fisheries Commission issued its report.

For the people of Keatley Creek, so utterly dependent on the river's bounty, such an ecological catastrophe would have been devastating. They could not wait for stocks to rebuild. With their stores of dried fish exhausted and no prospect of fresh supplies in sight, they had little choice but to abandon hearth and home. Bundling up their liquid assets—their necklaces and jade axes—noble families could have set off to the homes of their allies, assured of a warm welcome. But the poor, with little more than the bark clothes on their backs, had little to offer in exchange for hospitality. "That," says Hayden nodding, "would be a much bigger problem."

But tonight, under a sky speckled with stars, the specter of their desperation seems far away. Setting down his pipe, Hayden leans down and unlatches a well-worn violin case. Lifting out a gleaming fiddle, he tucks it into the crook of his neck and tests its tuning. As the campfire blazes, he taps his feet and saws out an old-time reel. In the ghostly quiet of the village, the rousing notes spill down over the hillside and into the river of night.

5

TRUE BELIEVERS

Hopeton Earthworks, Ohio

The first sanctuary is this earth.

—PLOTINUS

T he scene is one of faded glory, but glory nonetheless. On an August morning so new and fresh that dew glistens in the fields, drenching all in lush color, Mark Lynott and I peer out the window at a gentle roll of land just north of Chillicothe. Along the quiet country road beside us, morning glory threads the grasses in a wild tangle of alabaster blooms; trumpet vine, escaped from some long-vanished farmhouse garden, splashes fence posts with brilliant orange. But ahead, in the newly mown field, nature is trimmed and tamed. Lynott, a tall, husky midwesterner with a boyish thatch of straight dark hair, hunches over the steering wheel and gazes into the distance, arms crossed. "Right here in front of us," he says finally, pointing a finger to a barely perceptible swell of land, "you can see a little bit of rise where the hay is piled up. That's one of the walls."

We have come here this morning, Lynott and I, to see one of the fragile mysteries of North American archaeology—an immense geometric riddle known as Hopeton Earthworks. Built more than a millennium and a half ago and battered by modern plowshares, the massive earthen maze has nearly tumbled. But in the early morning light, shadows outline its surviving mounds. I follow Lynott's gaze. Directly ahead of where we sit, he explains, 12-foot-high earthen walls once framed a giant square: more than 100 grassy baseball diamonds could have nestled comfortably inside. Nearby, another great wall measuring 40 feet wide inscribed a huge circle. In the distance, two parallel embankments coursed straight and true—as if drawn with the edge of some gargantuan ruler—for nearly half a mile southwest to the floodplain of the Scioto.

Sitting here in the early morning light, envisioning this great maze, I am humbled. Like the famous standing stones of Europe—the menhirs of Brittany or Stonehenge in England—Hopeton reaches out beyond the strict confines of time and place. Translating faith, belief, and knowledge into the pure beauty of geometry, it transcends generations and cultures. And Hopeton was no mere isolated work. Less than a mile north of here stood another collosal square enclosure, Cedar Banks; to the east, just across the Scioto, lay the earthen edifices of Mound City. "What's so spooky," says Lynott, shaking his head solemnly, "is how many of these things existed at one time." Indeed, nearly two dozen of these geometric wonders—combinations of circles, half circles, squares, octagons, straight lines, and a miscellany of mounds and embankments—once graced the river valleys of southern Ohio. In one twelve-mile strip of the Scioto River alone, eight of these works crowned the terraces.

Exquisitely engineered, these enigmatic mounds enjoyed an early public fame, arousing much scientific curiosity. "What surprized me," wrote researcher Caleb Atwater in the early 1800s after poring over the enclosures at Circleville, "is the exact manner in which they had laid down their circle and square; so that after every effort, by the most careful survey, to detect some errour in measurement, we found that it was impossible, and that the measurement was much more correct, than it would have been, in all probability, had the present inhabitants undertaken to construct such a work" (Silverberg

Two views of the earthworks at Mound City, the Hopewell Culture National Historical Park. (Courtesy of the author.)

1968). Eager to discern their purpose, local scholars descended on the works with shovels and pickaxes. Sinking shafts and slicing trenches, they were soon struck with wonder. Embedded in many of the conical mounds were relics of strange unknown rites: charred human bones, clay-lined crematory basins, and fragments of haunting finery.

Indeed, the beauty of the finds was stunning—delicately carved effigy pipes, pearl necklaces and mantles, handwoven robes, copper headdresses shaped like deer antlers, repoussé copper plates, ceremonial blades of obsidian, copper earspools, shimmering mica cutouts of human hands and torsos, delicately incised bone and shell, ritual offerings of rare and handsome materials, meteoric iron, galena, fossil ivory, and fossil shark teeth. Nothing quite like these troves had ever been seen in North America before. Scientists were astonished. Unwilling to believe that ancestral native tribes wrought such wonders, antiquarians scoured biblical texts and rooted through the dusty chronicles of Spanish explorers for clues to the Mound Builders. Were they wandering Toltecs? Phoenicians? Or perhaps a lost tribe of Israel?

So heated did the controversy become that officials at the Smithsonian Institution in Washington finally bowed to public pressure, founding a Division of Mound Exploration. Dispatching a small platoon of scientists into the field, division head Cyrus Thomas sifted through their reports, weighing the findings for more than a decade before issuing his classic report on the subject in 1894. No lost races, he concluded, had slaved to build the earthworks: The engineers were ancestors of native tribes in eastern North America. "The links directly connecting the Indians and the mound-builders are so numerous and well established," concluded Thomas, "that archaeologists are justified in accepting the theory that they are one and the same people" (Thomas 1894).

Indeed, researchers now agree that the great earthen circles and squares of southern Ohio were inscribed some 1,500 to 2,200 years ago by the Hopewell, a people whose origins lay deep in the Ohio River valley. Named by archaeologists after a nineteenth-century landowner, the Hopewell espoused a po-

Hopewell artistry from Mound City: top, a pipe carved in the form of a bird; middle, a peregrine falcon made of copper; bottom, an obsidian blade (middle) and spear points. (Courtesy of the National Park Service.)

tent blend of religious, social, and political ideas that suddenly caught fire along the eastern half of the continent around 200 B.C. Developing a distinctive style of art and a common vocabulary of symbols, they spread their message far and wide for nearly 700 years, winning converts as far afield as the eastern edges of the Great Plains, the Atlantic seaboard, the Great Lakes, and the Gulf Coast. "I think there was a tremendous amount of ritual," says Hopewell scholar N'omi Greber, curator of archaeology at the Cleveland Museum of Natural History, "and a tremendous amount of ceremony."

But while much is known of Hopewell art and funerary practices, little has come to light of Hopewell lives. And Greber and many others now worry that time is slipping away. Across southern Ohio, industrial and residential developments gobble up the giant earthworks, many of which stretch over hundreds of acres; mechanized plows pound surviving mounds into oblivion. As the ancient riddles vanish, researchers scramble to answer a multitude of questions: Who exactly were the Hopewell? What drove them to raise such massive earthworks? What form did their society take? Were they reclusive farmers? Sociable villagers linked in an intricate political tapestry? And what lay at the heart of their powerful religion?

No one is more conscious of the ticking clock than tall, slow-speaking Mark Lynott, my companion this morning at Hopeton Works. A regional archaeologist with the National Park Service, Lynott has spent much of his professional career battling to protect the earthworks here. Fighting off a wicked cold this morning, the forty-five-year-old researcher stuffs a neatly folded handkerchief back in his pocket. He is clearly suffering, but there is no mistaking the conviction in his voice. "These big earthworks are just so damned haunting," says he quietly, shaking his head. "There's nothing else like them. They're just incredible."

An amiable man of 6 feet 4 with a broad, open face and a wealth of homespun wisdom, Lynott knows of what he speaks. A past president of the Society of Professional Archaeologists and the holder of a doctoral degree in anthropology from Southern Methodist University, he is intimately familiar with the archaeology of the Midwest. Campaigning quietly behind the scenes, he has rallied powerful allies to his cause. In 1992, to the amazement of many Ohio researchers, Congress agreed to buy what remains of four prominent earthworks—Hopeton, High Bank, Hopewell Mound, and Seip. Together with Mound City, already protected by the Park Service, these eerie earthen monuments will become the heart of a new Hopewell Culture National Historical Park.

Still, as Lynott is quick to point out, there is little time for savoring victory. "We've got 150 years of research but the questions are greater now than ever." To nail down answers, the Nebraskan researcher and his associates at the Park Service have embarked on a major new research program along the Scioto, enlisting specialists in fields as diverse as geophysics and mass spectrometry. Without doubt, they have their work cut out for them. At Hopeton, for example, the fields surrounding the great walls have yet to be systematically explored; the walls themselves stand undated and unstudied. To make up for lost time, Lynott has brought a crew of five to the southwest end of Hopeton for preliminary fieldwork.

Pulling up to the dig, he clambers out of his rented car, polishing off the last of a sizable bottle of Coca-Cola. Reaching for his fanny pack, he leads the way across a field to the edge of Hopeton's parallel walls. Beside us, crew members haul shovels and other gear to the pits like a straggling line of ants. The mood is convivial, but the irony of the location is lost on no one. Just a few hundred yards away, in a cloud of dust, a giant crane belonging to Chillicothe Sand and Gravel Company begins stripping away yet another great slab of earth. Unwilling to part with the property for anything less than the mineral price of the gravel, the firm presses on, gouging out great craters in the land.

For Lynott and many others, such mining threatens key studies. Since the earliest days of Hopewell studies, he explains, scientists have strained for even the slenderest glimpse of a society so fond of grandeur. In most other parts of the world, monuments of such extravagance signaled the pres-

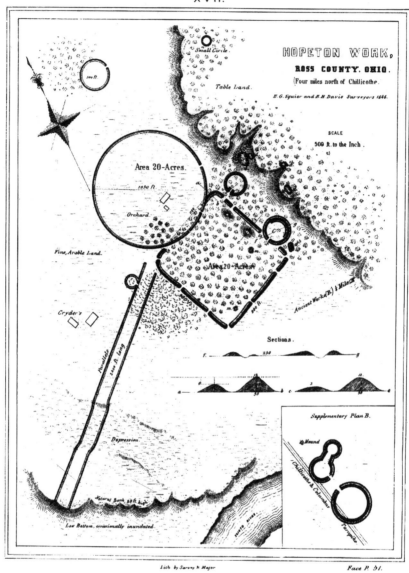

A *diagram of Hopeton Earthworks. (Reprinted from* Ancient Monuments of the Mississippi Valley, *E. G. Squier and E. H. Davis, 1848.)*

ence of elaborate civilizations. To erect the giant geometric earthworks here, suggested early scholars, the Hopewell needed overseers and sweating throngs, leaders and servile functionaries. How else could one account for such sophistication? "The Scioto River," concluded two early authorities, Ephraim Squier and Edwin Davis, "was a favourite resort of the ancient people and was one of the seats of their densest populations" (Squier and Davis 1848).

The great hitch is that researchers have unearthed little evidence of these throngs. Indeed, generations of scholars have failed to find even one major Hopewell village along the Scioto. At Mound City, for example, oral tradition held that Hopewell houses had once huddled beside the northern walls. So when the Park Service finally obtained title to the lands in the late 1970s, Lynott searched the area. With a small team, he walked the fields, combing the ground for broken flint tools and other refuse churned up by plowing. "We surveyed the entire length of it, up and down, up and down," he recalls. "And then in a few places where we found some Hopewellian materials, we excavated pits." But rumors of ruined houses proved figments: Only transient camps dotted the grounds.

Here at Hopeton, Lynott and his associates are again scouting for residences. Kneeling over three narrow test pits, crew members keep a sharp eye out for flaked stone, animal bone, the dark stain of a storage pit—anything that might herald human habitation. But they turn up little. A day in one of these pits yields only a few handfuls of tiny scraps—certainly not the rich seams of rubbish that characterize even the smallest hamlet. Such thin debris, says Lynott, points to a fleeting assembly of people who gathered at Hopeton for a few days at a time, then headed off somewhere else. "I'd say this is something of a seasonal-type base camp," he muses.

Just where they went from here is the million-dollar question. It's possible, says Lynott, that a Hopewell village lies buried on the floodplain or churned into tiny pieces in the dump heaps of the Chillicothe Sand and Gravel Company. Or perhaps the answer lies somewhere else entirely. Perhaps the Hopewell were a more reclusive folk.

✦   ✦   ✦

In the sultry afternoon heat, I sit in the shadows of a quiet patio, staring out at waving fields of corn and listening to Alva McGraw. A heavyset man in his mid-eighties, McGraw speaks in a soft torrent, filling in time with words and more words. A legend in these parts, McGraw moved to Chillicothe in the late 1930s and swiftly discovered a lifelong passion: archaeology. In the six decades that followed, he scrambled up terraces and bluffs and waded through swampy bottomlands, searching for traces of the Hopewell. No one knows this green countryside and its field archaeology better. And his memory is just short of photographic. For the last fifteen minutes, he has been recalling in vivid detail discoveries at the McGraw site.

In the early 1960s, a young Case Institute of Technology professor, Olaf Prufer, became fascinated by failed efforts to find a Hopewell village. The holder of a brand-new doctoral degree in anthropology from Harvard University, Prufer had read the scientific literature on such Maya centers as Copán, Palenque, and Tikal. During the 1950s, many scholars theorized that the great temples and plazas stood empty for most of the year. Their builders, they suggested, resided in scattered hamlets, tending to their fields of maize and other tropical crops. Only at certain times of the year—annual festivals or other great ritual occasions—did Mayan families gather in the stone splendor they had built.

Could the Hopewell have followed suit? Could they have planted maize, too, after obtaining seeds from southern peoples? Prufer thought it possible. And just outside Chillicothe, McGraw stumbled upon something that sounded interesting. While out working his fields, the burly farmer spied fragments of ceramic pots, marine shell, and flint tools strewn near an abandoned meander of the Scioto River. Prufer hustled out to take a look. Measuring just 10 square feet on the surface, the site looked tiny. But it lay directly in the path of a proposed highway. To retrieve what he could before the bulldozers appeared, Prufer reluctantly agreed to run a trench through the knoll. And as the team troweled down beneath the plow zone, they struck soil studded with shards. "It looked like a rubbish pit," says McGraw with a broad smile today. "So we began to dig it."

Perfectly preserved by annual blankets of silt from the Scioto River, the dense midden soon began yielding its humble quotidian treasures—broken flint tools; splintered mollusk shells; butchered deer, rabbit, and turkey bones; blackened hickory nuts, walnuts, and acorns; and a few kernels of maize, enough to suggest that the Hopewell had indeed farmed the crop. Even now, more than three decades later, McGraw smiles at the memory. He takes my pen and draws a map. "Prufer found a streak down here," he says, pointing a leathery finger to one spot, "and it was as dark as coal. It was full of artifacts and it was the prettiest thing I ever saw. It had fish bone, it had everything. It was the best site I ever worked in."

Radiocarbon tests revealed that residents had tossed out this rubbish around A.D. 450—during the last decades of the Hopewell building spree. And analysis suggested that people here had been deeply imbued with the Hopewell way of life. Not far from this midden, women had shaped clay into characteristic Hopewell vessels, decorating it in traditional Hopewell ways. Family members had knapped a profusion of flint bladelets like those unearthed in the Hopewell mounds. And some had busied themselves with fine arts and crafts, fashioning ceremonial goods from mica, bear teeth, and slate. The conclusion seemed inescapable. "Skilled hunters and food-collectors," wrote Prufer, "gifted artisans in a wide range of materials, the people who manufactured the rich grave goods for the ritual burials lived in small scattered farmsteads on the river bottoms" (Prufer 1964).

Still, it was just one site—not nearly enough to prove that the earthwork builders had all resided in such hamlets. And critics soon pounced. The corn kernels, for example, proved to be of much later origin. If the Hopewell were farmers, what crops did they plant? And where were their houses? For all the embarassment of riches at the McGraw site—10,000 shards, 6,000 animal bones, 2,000 mollusk shells—Prufer and his colleagues exhumed no dwellings. As the fallout settled, scholarly interest vanished until a small team of researchers led by Bill Dancey, a professor of archaeology at Ohio State University in Columbus, embarked on excavations along Raccoon Creek, two miles east of the most elaborate of all Hopewell constructions, Newark Works.

Perched above the creek, within easy reach of a now vanished marshland, the Murphy site looked rich in promise. "The flint along the ground was so massive after plowing," says Dancey, "there was just no mistaking it." And as team members began stripping off the plow zone in the early 1980s, the ghostly outlines of a small Hopewell homestead emerged from the loamy soil. Over the next three field seasons, excavators discovered fire-scorched hearths and soil stains left by the pole frames of one or two houses. Outside, they found earth ovens lined with charcoal and ash. Downslope lay the community rubbish dump.

Inhabited over a period of 300 years, until A.D. 200, this isolated homestead flourished at the very height of the Hopewell era. And microscopic scrutiny of its modest rubbish soon yielded an intimate glimpse into life among the Hopewell. Minute wear marks on their chert tools revealed that family members butchered fish and game, tanned and dressed animal hides, and whittled and engraved pieces of bone, antler, and stone. And the charred and blackened seeds that coated the earth ovens showed unmistakable signs of early agriculture. But the Hopewell, it transpired, were no slaves to imported maize. Indeed, those who tilled this terrace 2,000 years ago relied on no borrowed crops at all: Their ancestors had tamed their own.

✦   ✦   ✦

In the early eighteenth century, a restless French architect and engineer by the name of Antoine Le Page du Pratz strolled the communal gardens of the Natchez, a prosperous people who tilled the soils along St. Catherine Creek in present-day Mississippi. Well educated and adventurous, Le

Page du Pratz had won the friendship of the Natchez war chief, Tattooed Serpent, who gave the French scholar free rein to wander. In his rambles below the village, the curious engineer saw fields of corn, beans, and squash. And he took note of a lesser-known crop, a tall bushy plant whose sesame-sized seeds could be readily harvested each fall.

This obscure plant was *Chenopodium berlandieri* or goosefoot, and in the early 1980s it attracted the scholarly attention of Bruce Smith. A curator of North American archaeology at the Smithsonian Institution's National Museum of Natural History in Washington, Smith began delving into the origins of agriculture on the continent. An authority on the eastern woodlands, he noticed that seeds of the weedlike goosefoot flecked the botanical remains of many early sites along the Mississippi River and its northeastern tributaries. Had peoples in that region domesticated it long ago?

A lanky man with a long, narrow face and a bushy crescent-shaped mustache, Smith began casting around for ways of discerning ancient cultivation. In the 1970s, two agronomists at the University of Illinois found that domestication left minute hallmarks on modern plant seeds, altering both their size and structure. In the confines of a garden, noted Jack Harlan and Jan deWet, seedlings had to compete for one of the essentials of plant life—sunlight. The seeds that sprout first, thereby sending out leafy shoots that reap light and that shade rivals, survive. To do so, they need greater food supplies and much thinner seed coats—structural changes that can be seen and measured, thanks to electron scanning microscopy.

Intrigued, Smith began contacting colleagues, gathering samples of *Chenopodium berlandieri* seeds from prehistoric sites as far afield as Ohio, Kentucky, Alabama, and Missouri. "I started doing scanning electron microscope work to see if I could find any morphological evidence for their domesticated status," he says. Comparing seeds from modern stands of wild goosefoot with those from prehistoric sites dating back three millennia and more, Smith soon found some intriguing differences. Modern wild goosefoot seeds had coats 40 to 80 micrometers thick—about the width of a human hair: those from a 3,500-year-old Kentucky site possessed ones less than 20 micrometers thick. Clearly, says Smith, peoples of the eastern woodlands had begun planting these seeds as early as the second millenium B.C.

And goosefoot was not the only plant they sowed. Similar studies now show that they tamed marsh elder, sunflower, and an indigenous species of squash by about the same time, while more circumstantial evidence expands the list to include may grass, little barley, and erect knotweed. And what is fascinating, notes Smith, is that these early horticulturalists were sowing and reaping crops long before they ever laid eyes on maize or other agricultural imports. Peoples of the eastern woodlands embraced agriculture without the help of others. Indeed, Smith now ranks this region among the world's four independent, localized centers of plant domestication—along with the Near East, China, and Mesoamerica.

But while archaic peoples were the first to sow plants north of the Rio Grande, it was the Hopewell who first saw the greater possibilities of cultivation. In fact, says Smith, the rise of Hopewell groups coincides almost exactly with the advent of farming in the eastern woodlands. While earlier peoples had favored small occasional plots, Hopewell families began planting gardens and fields with these crops. The seeds of domesticated goosefoot and its kin, for example, abound in Hopewell sites; so, too, do tools for clearing the land. "It's difficult to get a handle on what level of dependence they had on their cultivated crops," says Smith, "or on how large their fields were and how much of their annual food intake was based on the crops. But I tend to think that they were pretty stable farmers and getting a fair amount of their nutrition from these crops."

Such native plants, after all, had much to offer. As little as three acres planted in goosefoot and marsh elder could yield half the calories needed by ten people for six months. And Hopewell families could harvest these fields relatively easily in fall. Goosefoot, for example, produces heavy clusters of tiny seeds. With little more than gathering-baskets in hand, a family could quickly strip the seeds from the stalks, then carry them home for drying and winnowing. "And probably what they did at that point was put them onto a grinding stone or into a pestle of some sort, and break the seed coat," notes Smith. "They could pound this into a paste or mix it in with a stew, or they may have made it into a trail mix."

At the small Hopewell homestead excavated by Bill Dancey and his team along the banks of Raccoon Creek, residents clearly grew such crops and relished such meals. Among the many seeds recovered from the earth ovens, archaeobotanist Dee Anne Wymer identified domesticated goosefoot and may grass, erect knotweed, marsh elder, and sunflower. To me, it seems increasingly clear that these small seeds held the kernels of Hopewell culture. By sowing and reaping, the Hopewell amassed comfortable stores of food, which provided time to reflect, contemplate the universe, conceive complex rituals, and construct an earthen geometry that stands today.

✦　✦　✦

On a late Friday afternoon, Bradley Lepper and I skirt the edges of an earthen wall in Newark, Ohio, our voices softened to a low hush. Over the past hour or so, Lepper, an archaeologist with the Ohio Historical Society, has been leading me down back alleys and across front yards as he points out remnants of Newark Works. Sprawling over four square miles, Newark is the largest set of geometric earthworks that the Hopewell constructed: Its giant square, octagon, circles, and parallel walkways pop up in unexpected places all over town. At the moment, Lepper and I are skirting the beautifully preserved rim of a circle along a local golf green. A few feet away, men in bermuda shorts bend over their putters, oblivious to the ancient walls that ripple along the course.

As we pass the ruins, admiring their smooth lines, I ask Lepper if he thinks the Hopewell were obsessed with death. Their greatest monuments have yielded hundreds of human burials and grave goods so finely made that they take the breath away. Scientific literature on the Hopewell is replete with descriptions of mortuary facilities—charnel houses, crematory basins, burial crypts—and exhaustive discussions of the ways Hopewell people laid their dead to rest—bundle burials, extended burials, cremations. To the casual reader, it seems that the center of their emotional lives, the core of their powerful religious beliefs, resonated with rituals of mourning and grief.

Lepper, a thoughtful man with a mop of wavy brown hair and a ready smile, shakes his head. Such an impression, he says, arises mainly from the biases of nineteenth-century archaeologists. Eager to amass collections of copper repoussé falcons and shimmering mica cutouts for public museums across the country, early researchers gravitated toward the burial mounds and their reliable troves of grave goods, paying little heed to the other enclosures and embankments. But at Newark, says Lepper, the Hopewell interred their dead in only one small area of the sprawling earthworks. "I think there's a lot going on here that has nothing to do with the dead."

One modern survey of the walls here, for example, suggests that the Hopewell paid close attention to astronomy—particularly certain lunar events. As well as waxing and waning every twenty-eight days, the moon progresses through a more obscure cycle every 18.6 years, as its rising and setting points shift along the horizon. While mapping the massive circle-and-octagon enclosure at Newark, two Earlham College researchers discovered that the central axis pointed to fifty-two degrees east of north—the northern extreme rise point of the moon in its extended cycle. At High Bank Works near Chillicothe, a very similar circle-and-octagon enclosure reveals an axis aligned to the southern extreme rise point of the moon. And based on his studies of antiquarian records in the region, Lepper is now convinced that the Hopewell linked the two great earthworks—separated by more than sixty miles as the crow flies—by a set of parallel walls.

In 1820, he explains, Caleb Atwater published research on Newark Works and other local mounds in the *Transactions and Collections of the American Antiquarian Society*. According to Atwater, a set of parallel walls ran south from Newark Works as far as thirty miles into the countryside. Forty years later, two careful surveyors, James and Charles Salisbury, traced these walls six miles into the countryside before giving up the mapping. "But they said the walls were still going in a perfectly straight line," notes Lepper, "and that would be thirty-one degrees west of south. Well, if you take an Ohio map and put a dot here and draw a line following those, it points directly to the center of Chillicothe."

In all likelihood, says Lepper, an ancient sacred road once connected the constellation of earthworks at Chillicothe—High Bank Works, Hopeton, Mound City, and others—to the mammoth mounds at Newark. And he believes that Hopewell peoples journeyed this sacred road at key times in the lunar calendar, reaching their final destination just as the moon rose along its northernmost or southernmost extreme. "So every nine years," he says, "people might be going from Chillicothe up here to participate in rituals and watch the moon rise." Nine years later, they may have walked this road in the opposite direction to witness the southernmost extreme of the moon at High Bank Works.

The exact nature of the many and varied rites they performed at Newark and the other great earthworks will probably never be known. But some ceremonies clearly entailed great pageantry and spectacle. Many of the fine mica and copper ornaments bear tiny holes, as if their Hopewell owners had once sewn them to robes or attached them to standards carried at the head of a procession. And at least one scholar, anthropologist Robert Hall, an expert on the symbolism and religious traditions of the eastern woodlands, now believes that some Hopewell rites centered on creation dramas—reenactments of a sacred legend.

Among native peoples throughout North America and much of Eurasia, writes Hall in one paper, storytellers long told a remarkably similar tale of the beginning of the earth. While the details varied somewhat, the essentials remained pretty much the same. In the beginning, they told their audiences, all was water. To form dry land, some of the animals decided to fetch mud from beneath the water. In most versions of the story, a succession of creatures tries to retrieve this earth and fails, but finally one returns with a tiny piece of muck in its paw. This soil then expands into hills and valleys—the foundation of all earth. In some versions, an earth maker finally holds it still by skewering its four edges with water snakes or anchors.

So pervasive is the Earth Diver myth among tribal peoples in both the Old and New World that storytellers have likely told it for thousands of years. And Hopewell shamans and their initiates may well have reenacted it at some of the great earth mounds. In Illinois, Wisconsin, and Minnesota—the region that Hall is most familiar with—excavators have uncovered strange and very distinctive mantles of peat, muck, and creek-bed clays covering Hopewellian mound burials. All come from the bottom of lakes and wetlands. So it is quite possible, suggests Hall, that ceremonialists once dove for these muds and spread them over the sacred mounds, remembering Earth Diver's great feat. And other pieces of evidence support the theory. In Illinois, excavators have found Hopewellian bodies covered with mats pegged to the ground with bone skewers.

On the plains of North America, notes Hall, certain tribes reenacted parts of this creation myth during the Sun Dance—an annual rite to initiate young men in sacred knowledge and to renew the world and bring fertility to all things that gave life. It now seems eminently likely that the Hopewell performed a creation ritual with similar intents at their burial mounds. "It is not difficult," Hall writes, "to imagine the chain of associations which could have led to the linking of creation and mortuary ritual in the Eastern Woodlands and the threads of a relationship that one might be able to trace between initiation, mourning, and New Life ritual within the historic Sun Dance of the Plains" (Hall 1979).

Whether or not Hall is right about the nature of these rituals, it is clear that the great enclosures once guarded sacred ground. And as Lepper and I walk back slowly to my car, we talk about the appeal these great earthen shrines must once have had to the faithful. Within these walls, the Hopewell left copper from Lake Superior, obsidian from the Rocky Mountains, shells from the Gulf Coast. "And what comes out of Ohio is just dribbles," says Lepper, clearly perplexed, "bits and pieces of Flint Ridge flint found in scattered areas—certainly not enough to account for any kind of even exchange. So maybe these places are like Mecca or the Vatican. Maybe people are coming from all over to participate in the mystery, to be part of it, to give their offerings and then go home with a new vision of life."

✦   ✦   ✦

As the sun begins to slip down the glazed horizon, I gather up notebooks and scientific papers and slide them into my briefcase. Sitting alone at a picnic table in the giant circle at Newark, I gaze around me at the swelling earth. A grassy wall curves sinuously into the distance like a great green eel, smooth, muscular, and taut. Trees poke from its sides like bristles. These walls seem strangely alive, effortlessly winding into the distance with their age-old secrets. Caught in their coil, I feel strangely at ease. For the moment, the outside world is banished; only the voices of children playing in the trees breaks the calm.

As I sit here, I recite a riddle that Lepper has told me. This circle that surrounds me is nearly a perfect circle, written large. The length of its circumference exactly equals the perimeter of the square that once rose north of here. That square was a perfect square. The circle over at the circle-and-octagon enclosure is a perfect circle. Its circumference is identical to that of the circle at High Banks and the inner circle at Circleville. And if one placed the small circle here at Newark inside the large circle, they would exactly match the two circles that gave Circleville its name. And so it goes. Maze within maze within maze.

I give up finally. I know I will never understand the intricacy of this geometry. And I remember something that Bill Dancey told me. "At other mysterious places," he said, "the solution is in the works. Like the Mayan collapse, for example, there's so much information on that now it's pretty clear that it wasn't a collapse and it wasn't the product of an invasion. So you can talk very confidently about what the society was like." He paused. "But Hopewell," he said, finally shrugging, "still a mystery."

6

DESERT PROPHETS

Chaco Canyon, New Mexico

*One might regard architecture as history
arrested in stone.*

—A. L. ROWSE

Tom Windes beckons. Balanced on a narrow stone ledge, I turn and back down the ladder, sweeping loose a fine cloud of dust, droppings, and cactus spines. In the dimness below, the silent researcher turns and holds up the light, casting a strange surreal glow over centuries of abandonment. All around us, 3-foot-thick masonry walls rise to the ceiling, walling out the day. In the far corner, a pair of bats circle frantically in the air before departing into the gloom. Windes, a National Park Service archaeologist, shrugs, reaching for his battered toolbox. We are standing in the subterranean heart of Chetro Ketl, a sprawling 500-room greathouse built more than 900 years ago in the New Mexico desert. I am mesmerized.

Outside, it is an early fall morning in remote Chaco Canyon, a rugged sandstone scar that runs for twenty miles across the bleak barrens of the San Juan Basin. Already the sun has burned off tendrils of haze, warming northern cliffs. But here in this ancient greathouse, one of more than a dozen such huge masonry buildings preserved in Chaco Culture National Historical Park, time stands still. As Windes rifles through the toolbox, hauling out tape measures, levels, and charts, I roam the far corners of the room. In the shadows, patches of gray plaster still cling to sandstone walls, resisting the ruin of a millennium. Along the sandy floor, dozens of dead rabbits sprawl in the dust, staring out balefully from the gloom.

Windes has brought me here this morning to help map walls and measure roof beams in a never-excavated section of Chetro Ketl. To work in the underground rooms, we have donned gas masks, a protective measure against the hantavirus that has recently swept parts of the Four Corners. Carried by rodents and spread in rodent droppings, hantavirus frequently ends in respiratory failure. There is no known cure. To my eyes, these clunky gas masks seem a quaint form of defense, but I sincerely hope they are working. The floors inside this greathouse are lined with mouse droppings. Along one wall, a dead mouse withers in the sand. "It was alive the last time I was here," says Windes dryly. "I saw it kicking around."

Yet for all the dust, death, and decay, many North American archaeologists would give just about anything to sift through this debris. For more than a century now, science has stood in awe of the greathouses of Chaco Canyon. Rising as high as five stories in the air and stretching for tens of thousands of square feet in intricately planned grids of rectangular rooms and round chambers, these stunning masonry buildings represent the most elaborate, and many would say the most beautiful, architecture in all prehistoric North America. "It's like the Emerald City of Oz of its time," notes Stephen Lekson, president of Crow Canyon Archaeological Center in Cortez, Colorado, and an expert on Chaco architecture. "There's nothing else like it in the Southwest."

Such grandeur is all the more impressive given the setting. Receiving just 9 inches of precipitation in an average year, Chaco Canyon is a wilderness of saltbush, snakeweed, and prickly pear, favored mainly by mice and lizards. Trees are rare and water is at a premium—conditions that have prevailed for more than 1,000 years. Yet in such hostile terrain, canyon dwellers embarked on a building spree that lasted more than a

Aerial view of Chetro Ketl. (Courtesy of the American Museum of Natural History.)

century. To construct just one room, calculates Lekson, crews quarried 50 tons of sandstone from neighboring cliffs and carted 16 tons of clay from canyon soils. To roof it, they carried forty or so wooden beams—some weighing as much as 600 pounds—from forests forty miles away or more. The oldest and largest greathouse, Pueblo Bonito (or "beautiful town" in Spanish), boasted nearly 800 of these rooms. Many are still standing today, 900 years after construction ended.

Careful study has shown that the stoneworkers who built these greathouses were Anasazi, prehistoric pueblo people who cultivated corn and other crops across much of the Four Corners region. But at Chaco Canyon they clearly outdid themselves. Along the mesas and sidewashes, archeologists have discovered an astonishing variety of architecture—from small shrines and huge circular masonry chambers known as great kivas to plazas, roads, and prosperous agricultural villages. And the influence of the canyon rippled far and wide in the countryside, as masons raised Chacoan-style architecture in dozens of far-flung communities. Today, many experts suggest that

Shaped like a giant "D," Pueblo Bonito sprawls over the canyon floor. (Courtesy of the American Museum of Natural History.)

Chaco Canyon lay at the heart of a vast regional system—some say an early state—that sprawled over more than 60,000 square miles of the Southwest. By the middle of the eleventh century, writes Lekson in one paper, Chaco Canyon "probably was the primary settlement of the Anasazi world" (Lekson 1987).

But much, including the very purpose of the greathouses, remains mysterious. After excavating part of Pueblo Bonito during the 1920s, researcher Neil Judd concluded that the massive building once sheltered more than 1,000 people. "No other apartment house of comparable size," he wrote confidently in *National Geographic*, "was known in America or in the Old World until the Spanish Flats were erected in 1882 at 59th Street and Seventh Avenue in New York" (Judd 1925). But modern researchers are far less sanguine. While digs at Pueblo Bonito turned up a wealth of ceremonial gear—obsidian arrowheads, painted wooden flutes, pottery pipes, ceramic human effigies, birds carved from hematite, frogs carved of jet and inlaid with turquoise—they disclosed scarcely a trace of domestic life. Subsequent work at the greathouses of Chetro Ketl, Una Vida, and Kin Kletso revealed just one empty room after another.

In light of such findings, researchers now grapple with a host of troubling questions. What kind of a capital, they wonder, was Chaco Canyon? Why did canyon dwellers go to such elaborate lengths to build so many greathouses? Were they shrines to a powerful religious cult? Private palaces or warehouses? Or could they have served a variety of purposes? And just how did canyon residents come to wield such influence over the countryside? What became of the people of Chaco in the end?

Windes, for one, would dearly love to know the answers. In the bright afternoon sunlight, the tall, gaunt archaeologist kneels down along a warren of low sandstone walls, flipping on the switch of a small black receiver. In the distance, a Navajo rancher slowly cruises the dirt road in a gleaming pickup truck, searching for missing cattle. But Windes is intent on the work at hand. Beneath his feet lies the stony skeleton of a greathouse that he and colleagues John Schelberg and Art Ireland discovered just nine years ago along the eastern fringes of the canyon. Draped in windblown sediment and known as Place Where the Red Ants Have Left, the mammoth building has yet to be fully mapped, much less studied and published. As Windes waits for the receiver to record coordinates of latitude and longitude from a global positioning satellite, he interprets the lay of the land. "All those things over there are small houses," he explains, pointing out a scattering of low mounds in the distance that once constituted a bustling Anasazi village. "And there's the prehistoric road. See how they dug it all out?"

A veteran field archaeologist with a fine eye for detail, Windes has been studying greathouses and roads for more than two decades now. In the early 1970s, researchers in the region became intrigued by a network of arrow-straight lines radiating out from the canyon. "There was quite a bit of issue

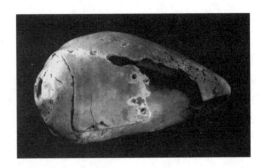

Vestiges of life at Pueblo Bonito: top, a shell trumpet; bottom left, a sandal; bottom right, a ceramic human head. (Courtesy of the American Museum of Natural History.)

Jacques Cinq-Mars stands by a shadowy cave entrance at Bluefish Caves in the northern Yukon. (Courtesy of the author.)

Painted figures tower along the back wall of Panther Cave in Texas. (Copyright Robert W. Parvin.)

*A yellow-robed shaman seems to beckon observers at Panther Cave.
(Courtesy of the author.)*

The White Shaman rises along a rocky wall in the Lower Pecos. (Courtesy of the author.)

A view of the Keatley Creek site, looking toward the Fraser River Canyon. The outlines of house pits can be seen midfield in the picture. (Courtesy of Brian Hayden.)

Prehistoric earthworks ripple across the landscape at Mound City.
(Courtesy of Harper San Francisco.)

One section of Newark Works stands out clearly after a snowfall. (Courtesy of the National Park Service.)

Golden light bathes Chaco Canyon and the semicircular ruin of Pueblo Bonito. (Courtesy of Facts On File.)

Beneath the high terraced slopes of Monks Mound (upper center), the grand plaza of Cahokia sprawls for nearly forty acres. Dozens of smaller earthen mounds surround the plaza. (Courtesy of Melvin Fowler.)

More than 100,000 bison met their end at the cliffs of Head-Smashed-In Buffalo Jump in Alberta. (Copyright Thomas Kitchen.)

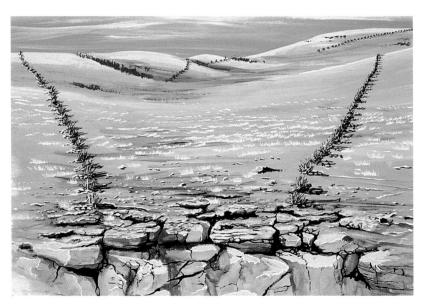

Drive lanes, such as those illustrated above, once helped to funnel bison herds to the lethal cliff edge. (Courtesy of the Provincial Museum of Alberta.)

going on over whether these were prehistoric roads or not," says Windes. With aerial photographs in hand, archaeologists from the Bureau of Land Management and other agencies set out into the field. Walking remote desert washes, they found mysterious swales wider than modern two-lane highways. Scooped out from the ground and speckled in spots with ancient pottery shards, several stretched as far as the eye could see. The longest, the Great North Road, climbed elaborately carved stairways in the cliffs behind Pueblo Bonito and ran for more than thirty miles north across the sun-scorched brush.

It was a fascinating find. But why had the Anasazi, a pedestrian culture that had never seen draft animals or wheeled carts, constructed nearly 200 miles of roads? "It certainly gave us pause to think," says Windes with a smile. Perhaps, suggested some, Chaco Canyon had flourished in the eleventh century as a bustling market, importing corn, timber, pottery, and other valuable commodities from far-flung corners of the Anasazi world. Setting up stalls in the shadows of the greathouses, merchants could have hawked their wares to buyers or barterers from the surrounding countryside, reaping the profits. While some greathouses may have served as spacious warehouses, others could have been built as residences for wealthy traders.

But hard evidence was slim. Early excavators in the canyon swept through the greathouses, throwing out or churning up much valuable data in their search for antiquities. "We didn't really understand what the rooms were like in the greathouses," explains Windes, shaking his head. To gather critical new evidence, researchers from the National Park Service decided to launch a modern excavation. The prime candidate was an eleventh century greathouse, Pueblo Alto. Perched along the northern rim of the canyon, it commanded a spectacular view of the San Juan Basin. And it had strong links with the road system: Seven prehistoric avenues, including the Great North Road, ran right past its walls.

Unable to excavate all of Pueblo Alto, Windes and his colleagues set to work carefully planning their attack. Clearing out the rubble from along buried walls, crew members spent months mapping rooms and analyzing architectural space. Poring over differences in size and location, they categorized the rooms and selected a small sample for exacavation. But as they scraped away the layers of roof fall and dirt, they were astonished by the eerie emptiness. Furnishings were absent; plastered floors were pristine. "It was like nobody had ever stepped foot in them, like they had been made yesterday," marvels Windes. "And you're going, what's this?"

As the work proceeded, the mystery deepened. Pollen samples taken from plastered floors yielded little trace of stored grains, fruits, or vegetables. Excavations in the plaza revealed no sign of commerce. "We imagined that we'd find a lot of postholes for stalls," says Windes, author of the three-volume final report on the site, "but we didn't find anything." More puzzling still were the strange contents of the trash mound. In place of the customary domestic debris—ash, charcoal, and cornstalks—crew members unearthed dense layers of chert flakes, butchered antelope and deer bones, and jagged pieces of pots. In all more than 150,000 cooking vessels and finely painted bowls had been dumped on the heap over sixty years—an astonishing rate of breakage. And unlike ordinary refuse, taken out daily or weekly, this garbage had been tossed out in great quantities just once a year or so.

After carefully considering the evidence, Windes now flatly dismisses speculations that Pueblo Alto ever housed hundreds of permanent residents. Of the eleven rooms excavated, only two revealed any clear sign of domestic life. In all likelihood, says Windes, no more than fifty people—caretakers or administrators—resided in the echoing complex. And it is highly improbable that the building ever served as a bustling marketplace. Research now shows that pottery and other goods did not flow through the canyon on their way somewhere else: Most were consumed or destroyed here.

In all likelihood, Pueblo Alto served a very different purpose—as a place of religious pilgrimage. Sheltering a small number of caretakers or important people for most of the year, concludes Windes, the greathouse stirred to life for just a few brief days annually, welcoming hundreds of people from villages in the canyon and surrounding countryside. Taking shelter in Pueblo Alto, the pilgrims feasted, danced, and destroyed vast quantities of valuable ceramics in sacred ritual. "Year in and year out, a lot of people showed up and threw away a lot of stuff," concludes Windes, climbing back into the truck. "Something was going on there."

✦　✦　✦

The next morning as I drive along the canyon's rutted gravel road, past crumbling shells of greathouses and a land desolate in its silence, I think about these ancient pilgrims and the journey that brought them here. In the distance, cliffs the color of old bone tilt over rocky slopes, weathering slowly to dust. Faded-green brush carpets the broad canyon floor. The sky has a hard turquoise gleam. In such a parched land, people always struggled from rainfall to rainfall. To survive, they lived on faith. Yet they left us no clear testament of their beliefs, no codices, scrolls, or stelae. In a culture without written language, their voices have vanished; archaeologists roll in an agony of questions.

But some clues remain. Along the rocky summit of Fajada Butte, a small steep-sided mesa guarding the southern entrance of the canyon, Anna Sofaer and her team have uncovered tantalizing records of sacred ceremony. An authority on Anasazi astronomy and the head of the Solstice Project in Washington, D.C., Sofaer now struggles to decipher the meaning. "We're trying to understand what consumed the mental and emotional passions of the people here—what their art was, what their religion was," she explains. "We can never know the specifics, but we can certainly know what consumed a lot of mental energy and social focus."

Sofaer began her research in the late 1970s, while recording a series of rock-art images—spirals, rectangle forms, and an undulating snake—along the summit of Fajada Butte. Finishing up her notes one morning, she witnessed an unexpected display: Just before noon, a brilliant dagger of sunlight sliced between two overlying rock slabs, briefly striking near the center of the largest spiral. "I happened to be there within a minute or two, when it looked the strongest," she explains. "The dagger was centered in the spiral and the visual impact was tremendous." It was the last week in June, and Sofaer immediately recognized the significance. The spiral was a calendrical device for marking the summer solstice.

Similar spiral images dotted Anasazi rock art. And Sofaer had spied ancient-looking potsherds along the trail. Fascinated, she decided to study Fajada Butte more closely. Returning time and again over the next few years with colleague Rolf Sinclair, a physicist at the National Science Foundation in Washington, she discovered that sunlight illuminated other rock-art images on the butte during key astronomical events, too—most notably at noontime during the spring and fall equinoxes. It was a striking and repetitive pattern that puzzled both researchers. Why had Anasazi observers been so fascinated by the noontime position of the sun on these two days?

Perplexed, Sofaer turned to published accounts of modern Puebloan cultures for clues. Descended from the Anasazi, tribes such as the Hopi and the Zuni had steadfastly maintained age-old traditions. As Sofaer immersed herself in this literature, she was soon struck by a sacred story told by many Puebloan peoples. Among the Zuni, for example, elders spoke of a time when all humans and animals were sealed in an underworld of darkness. In the sky above, the sun had taken pity on their plight, creating two sons from the mists. With bow and arrow, the two brothers made a sacred hole in the earth known as the *shipapu,* and helped the humans to escape. But the trials of men and women were not yet over. According to many Puebloan accounts, the people wandered south for many years, until at last they settled in the Middle Place—the point on earth where north, south, east, and west all converged.

As she mulled over the story, Sofaer wondered if it could hold the key to markings on Fajada Butte. On the morning of the equinox, the sun rises at true east; in the evening, it sets at true west. And at noon on those two days of the year, it lies along an imaginary line stretching from true north to true south. For a few brief minutes then, the sun seems to crown the very center of the sky—a place where the four cardinal directions converge. "It's middle of the year, middle of the day, middle of time," says Sofaer. "And the cardinal directions are thought of as middle, too—Middle Place."

It all seemed to fit, for Chaco builders encoded very similar spatial symbolism in some of the canyon's most important architecture. At Pueblo Bonito, masons constructed the long center wall of the greathouse along a true north-south line and the principal outer wall along a true east-west axis. Where the two structures joined, the cardinal directions intersected—an earthly Middle Place. And masons paid similar attention to the compass while constructing Casa Rinconada, a great kiva. The Solstice Project team was fascinated. Had the Anasazi once regarded Chaco Canyon as the Middle Place?

If such were the case, other monuments in the canyon might represent additional features of the sacred landscape. The Great North Road, for example, could lead to the ancient *shipapu*, the place in the ground where humans first emerged from the underworlds. It was an intriguing thought, impossible to prove, but Sofaer, Sinclair, and colleague Michael Marshall were keen to take a look. "It was just so striking that there was this elaborate road going out thirty-five miles north," Sofaer says.

Studying Bureau of Land Management photographs and walking long stretches, the team soon saw that the road followed a logic of its own. Crossing desert lands almost devoid of settlement—modern or prehistoric—it stretched 30 feet wide on average. In some spots, it formed two and even four parallel lanes before merging once again into one. And it seemed bereft of a practical purpose. As it stretched to its end, the team could find no trace of an Anasazi settlement. Instead, the road drew up to the rim of a great portal in the rock known as Kutz Canyon. An ancient wooden stairway littered with pottery shards descended to the bottom. "You really don't see what the canyon is until you are almost a hundred feet away," says Sofaer. "And then it just *fills* you with its emptiness. It's incredible."

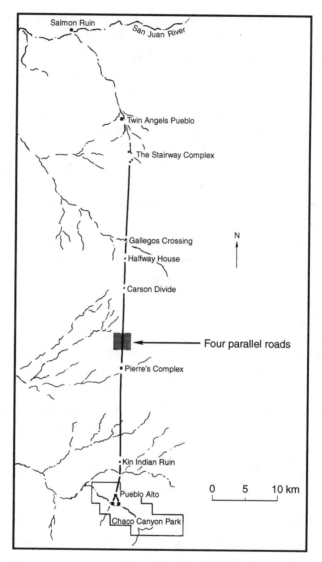

Map of the Great North Road. (Copyright The Solstice Project.)

To Sofaer, it now seems clear that the Great North Road was an expression of cosmology and religious faith. "In many of the pueblos," she explains, "north is regarded as a very important direction. It is held to be the origin of the people, where they came from the worlds below. It's also the place where the spirits of the dead return." In some pueblos, for example, grieving families leave offerings symbolizing the deceased in canyons to the north. In other pueblos, mourners place a last meal for the dead in a pottery vessel and break its rim, scattering the pieces in the direction of the *shipapu.*

And it is entirely possible that the Great North Road once served as a major route of pilgrimage. A hundred years ago at the pueblo of Acoma, for example, ceremonialists packed offerings to the sun on the backs of burros and journeyed for more than 150 miles north to the place where the ancestors first climbed out from the underworlds; at Zuni today, ritualists continue to make similar pilgrimages. And these reenactments of the ancient migration may explain one of the most puzzling features of the Great North Road: the multiple lanes. In some versions of the sacred story, migrants separate briefly into two and four clans before joining together again.

Whether Anasazi pilgrims traveled the Great North Road to honor their dead and revere their gods, says Sofaer, can never be proven. Nearly 900 years have passed between modern Puebloan people and their desert ancestors, and much may have changed. But as she sits in her Washington, D.C., office today, surrounded by thumb-worn maps and dog-eared architectural diagrams of greathouses, Sofaer is clearly struck by the parallels between past and present. And she marvels at the way Chacoan architects and engineers united time and space, science and art, cosmos and humanity in their work. "Most of it is organized in such a beautiful way," she says finally, a note of awe in her voice. "It goes so much beyond what would be needed to tune into seasonal cycles for planting crops."

✦   ✦   ✦

But on a gray overcast morning in early October, I am reminded that not all walked in harmony in this canyon. Wandering through the ragged maze of Pueblo Bonito, surrounded by crumbling walls that look apocalyptic in their shattered beauty, I mull over the theories of David Wilcox. A curator at the Museum of Northern Arizona in Flagstaff and an expert on the Hohokam culture of the American Southwest, Wilcox has spent seven years studying political organization and violence among the Anasazi. Today, he sees Chaco Canyon as the home of powerful rulers who dominated much of the countryside with a combination of ruthlessness and military might. "I've been led to some fairly radical ideas of these matters compared to where most other people are," he concedes when I talk to him later.

A thoughtful man with long, graying hair tied back in a thick ponytail, Wilcox began looking at Chacoan politics in the late 1980s, after listening to a colleague present a paper on the canyon's ancient climate. Struck by the generally arid conditions in the late eleventh century, Wilcox wondered why Chacoans had picked such a trying time to add 100,000 square feet of storage area to canyon greathouses. "Why are they building these huge structures down there in that god-forbidden place, putting all that labor into it? And it occurred to me, why not think about it as unequal exchange—tribute. They were building these structures to store tribute."

In considering the idea, Wilcox could see that the greathouses were similar in scale to the monumental architecture favored by early states. And certainly Chaco exerted a potent influence on the countryside. Perhaps, he reasoned, canyon dwellers and their closest neighbors formed a polity or city-state in the late tenth century, and began casting envious eyes on regions to the south. "They are much more fertile, productive lands," he says. With the help of warrior societies, he theorized, Chacoan rulers could well have marshaled several fighting forces of forty or so men. They would be small but effective. "If they show up at a village of 200 and say, 'we want the goods,' what are the people going to do? They are going to say yes."

Certainly the theory might explain why distinctive Chacoan architecture sprang up across the Four Corners in the eleventh century. But was there any evidence of such coercion? Curious, Wilcox began poring through the scientific literature. In dozens of Anasazi sites, field archaeologists stumbled on strange charnel pits and rooms scattered with charred and broken human bones. Bearing little sign of traditional burial practices, these pits looked much like the mass graves so common in war-ravaged countrysides. Indeed, the strange finds had aroused the suspicions of several physical anthropologists. Poring over the bones with hand lenses and floodlamps, researcher Christy Turner and others examined their surfaces carefully. Along some, they noticed cut marks from stone tools, abrasions from hammerstones, and a telltale polish that resulted from stirring bones in a pottery vessel— troubling signs of cannibalism. In other graves, they found fractured skulls, smashed jaws, and arrowheads embedded in bone. In all, more than 470 men, women, and children had succumbed to acts of violence and cannibalism at forty different sites.

Such ruthlessness seems little in keeping with the peaceful lives of Puebloan peoples today. But at critical times in their history, notes Wilcox, they resorted to brutal force. At the beginning of the eighteenth century, for example, Hopi leaders executed a devastating attack on the Hopi village of Awatovi, which had converted to Roman Catholicism. Sweeping down on the pueblo, warriors killed many of its 800 inhabitants and cannibalized some as a clear warning to others. In the countryside surrounding Chaco Canyon, Anasazi warriors may have simply done the same. "It fits the idea that these people are going out and coercing people not doing what they want them to do," he explains. "They're treating them like animals. It's not food, it's a political message: 'Don't screw around with us or you'll be desecrated and devastated.' "

More important still, he adds, this ancient slaughter took place just as Chacoans were feverishly building roads and outlier greathouses. Did rulers at Chaco Canyon orchestrate such mayhem, calling the shots from greathouse corridors? Wilcox hunted for clues. And as he studied the reports on Pueblo Bonito, he was struck by the lavish burials of two men in one of the oldest parts of the greathouse. One had been draped with strings of turquoise beads and laid to rest with seashells from the coast of California. At his side lay a turquoise-encrusted basket filled with turquoise beads. The grave goods were telling. Researchers had exhumed similar objects from the tomb of another male in Arizona; Hopi elders identified them as the belongings of a war leader and a chief responsible for dealings with the world at large.

With bands of well-trained warriors drawn both from the canyon and from neighboring areas, notes Wilcox, Chacoan war leaders could have quickly overpowered defenseless farming communities. Sending out a territorial chief or recruiting a local agent to their cause, they may then have swiftly set the gears of state in motion. Before long, canyon masons appeared to build a Chacoan greathouse for storing tribute and a Chacoan great kiva for holding rituals of the state religion. "It's pretty obvious that this religious ideology was real important to how this worked," he notes. "You can readily see that it acted in some way to legitimize all of these claims."

And for nearly a century, Wilcox theorizes, the Chacoan way of life ruled. Wealth in the form of corn, turquoise, obsidian, jet, shell, copper, and macaw feathers streamed into the canyon. Construction crews toiled. The greathouse of Chetro Ketl, suggests Wilcox, may have served as a lavish palace for the canyon leadership; Pueblo Bonito could have been dedicated to the state cult. And hundreds of rooms were likely added to greathouses to store the small mountains of tribute. But as the twelfth century unfolded, resistance began to mount. To the north, leadership rivals installed themselves in a magnificent new greathouse at Aztec. To the south, outlying settlements rebelled, launching what Wilcox sees as a series of successful revolts. "In a tribute system, if you say forget it, I'm not going to pay anymore, and they come and you successfully resist them, you're independent."

Moreover, studies by other scholars suggest that nature itself was preparing a heavy blow. In 1130, the rain stopped falling in northwestern New Mexico; it did not return to normal patterns for fifty years. Throughout Chaco Canyon, cornfields withered, construction ceased, and hopes died. Little by little, canyon families gathered up their belongings and scattered to higher lands in the north and south—anywhere that patches of green still survived. By 1150, suggest most experts, the canyon was virtually deserted: Only an occasional pilgrim stood before the greathouse doors.

✦   ✦   ✦

But was this the end of the Chacoan faith? Was all of its influence lost? As he gazes down on a deep-green slope some eighty miles north of Chaco Canyon, Bruce Bradley smiles and shakes his head. A small, weathered man in dusty jeans and battered felt hat, Bradley has spent the past decade studying Sand Canyon Pueblo, a massive thirteenth-century village tucked away from sight in the piñon pines and juniper of southern Colorado. Just a week away now from completing his field research and backfilling the 40 or so rooms excavated in the sprawling 400-room complex, Bradley believes that he and his team have uncovered traces of a last, desperate stand by a Chacoan messiah.

A senior research scientist at the Crow Canyon Archaeological Center in Cortez, Bradley began excavations at the pueblo in the early 1980s, eager to uncover answers to an old archaeological riddle. For reasons unknown, Anasazi families in southwestern Colorado had embraced a major change in the thirteenth century. Abandoning their small farmsteads around 1250, they began retreating to large pueblos hidden away at the heads of canyons or beneath the rims of cliffs, in places such as the world-famous Mesa Verde National Park. Just what lay behind this sudden penchant for isolation and secretiveness was far from clear, but as Bradley and his crew lifted layers of mud and dirt from the walls at Sand Canyon Pueblo, they began to glimpse some fascinating clues.

Occupied for just thirty-five years after construction began around 1250, the horseshoe-shaped pueblo exhibited a striking town plan. Along the eastern half of the site, Anasazi families built a strip of private dwellings similar to the small houses of Chacoan villages. Along the western side, they constructed a broad public plaza edged by a sturdy two-storied building that looked much like a miniature Chacoan greathouse. Indeed with its D-shaped floor plan, it looked startlingly like a very particular greathouse. "This is Pueblo Bonito," says Bradley with a smile. And the resemblances to Chaco Canyon did not stop there. A short distance away, on a steep slope, residents had raised the wall of a great kiva—a century after construction of these structures had ceased elsewhere in the region.

To Bradley, it seemed clear that families here had religiously preserved the memory of Chaco Canyon for more than 100 years and faithfully transposed its essential architectural templates—greathouse and great kiva—to the Colorado forest. And other families in the region had done much the same. As the Cambridge University–trained archaeologist searched through the sketchy scientific literature on thirteenth-century pueblos in the region, he could see that several featured similar design elements, including the miniature greathouse. "We're finding more of these D-shaped buildings the more we look at these late canyon-head sites," he says.

In light of this evidence, Bradley now suggests that many if not all of these remote canyon pueblos were built by like-minded souls—followers of a strict religious cult. Building villages hidden away from sight, they seem to have deliberately removed themselves from the mainstream, much the way modern-day cults such as the Branch Davidians prefer doing. "My interpretation at this point is that we're seeing a reactionary, fundamentalist, charismatic religious movement based on a vision of an individual or a small group of individuals," says Bradley, watching a low cloud of white mist move up the canyon. "And what's the premise? Chaco. I'm saying we have a Chacoan revivalist movement probably equivalent in strength to the Ghost Dance of the 1870s."

Born in troubled times when traditional values were eroding as Europeans settled the Great Plains, the Ghost Dance religion of the Sioux and others harked back to a happier period when they hunted the great herds of bison. And a similar wave of religious revivalism may have swept parts of the Southwest in the thirteenth century. Throughout the region, radical change was brewing. In pueblos along the Rio Grande to the south, people observed new rites honoring masked gods and ancestral spirits, giving birth to what is today called the kachina cult. But at Sand Canyon and elsewhere in the Mesa Verde region, residents clung to the old ways, keeping Chacoan symbolism alive. "To me, the compelling part of the argument is that it's such a basic thing that humans do in a state of confusion," says Bradley. "Things aren't seeming to work out, you're drifting psychologically, emotionally, religiously. There's just an incredible urge to go back to the good old days."

Just who led the revival movement is far from clear, but Bradley suggests an important clue may lie at Sand Canyon. While clearing debris from the west side of the pueblo, team members discovered remains of a middle-aged male with a rare genetic trait: six toes. Bradley had seen a striking reference to that trait in Chaco Canyon itself. In a small ceremonial room behind Pueblo Bonito, petroglyphs of two six-toed feet climbed toward the heavens. And in the inner sanctum of the greathouse itself, excavators had uncovered the disturbed burial of a person with six toes—"exactly identical to the one we have here," says Bradley.

Did some Anasazi regard the birth of a six-toed boy in the thirteenth century as a sacred sign? And could some have later followed a young man with this auspicious deformity into remote canyons of southern Colorado and Utah to found a new cult? While Bradley concedes the idea is purely speculative, the dates are suggestive. "I would think if the six-toed person was considered something special or symbolic in Chacoan times," he says, "a little baby born in the early 1230s with those six toes would have been set aside as special." And by the 1250s, a decade when many of the large cliffside pueblos in the region are built, this young man would have reached the age of majority—an ideal time to become a messiah.

With or without such a leader, however, Sand Canyon certainly set about cutting ties to the outside world. Dispensing with commerce and trade, its residents turned inward, removing themselves from the contagion of new ideas. And for twenty years or so, all went peacefully enough. But the people of Sand Canyon could not barricade themselves off entirely from the outside world. By 1270, ritualists in some ceremonial rooms had dispensed with the cylindrical pots long associated with Chacoan ritual. In their place, they used square and rectangular vessels. "And that's exactly what happened in the kachina cult," says Bradley. "You no longer have round kivas, you've got square kivas, rectangular kivas."

For Sand Canyon, it was clearly the beginning of the end. As southern ideas permeated the pueblo, bitter strife broke out—with deadly results. The six-toed man, for example, was slain with a blow to the head: His body was dumped in a small room. Other residents were slaughtered en masse. No longer united by a common spirit, the survivors packed up their most valuable possessions and set fire to their kivas. "And where they went," says Bradley finally, looking down at the strip of rectangular and circular rooms, "they didn't build these round kivas again."

As I walk through the cold, bright Colorado sunshine, heading back to my car, I think of the refugees and the trails of black smoke that streaked the skies behind them. Try as we will, we will never understand their fervor or grasp the faith that flourished in this forlorn land. Despite all our efforts, we will never speak the names of their prophets or recite the histories of their lords. After a century of research, Chaco still eludes us. In the walls of sandstone, we see only ourselves.

7

LORD OF THE BLACK DRINK

Cahokia, Illinois

The object of power is power.

—GEORGE ORWELL

"The bodies were all over the place," he says finally. "It looked like they had stood on top and pitched them in like bottles." Al Meyer lapses into silence. A short, barrel-chested man with thinning gray hair and the labored breathing of one who has learned nearly all there is to know of heart trouble, he searches out my eyes, uncertain of the reaction. In the foyer beyond, a lone flute caresses the air, sweet and soothing; museum docents whisper in hushed voices. But Meyer refuses to be lulled. Reaching for my steno pad, he tips a pencil from his breast pocket and begins roughing in details of a 1,000-year-old execution. A swift oval serves as the pit; scrawls and stick figures convey the victims. "This one had the rib cage spread out," he says finally, tilting the paper for me to see. "I assume they removed some organ or another. One of the ones down here had a projectile point. This one was minus a head."

Meyer lays down the pencil. Beyond the window where we sit, heavy gray cloud stretches taut to the horizon, sealing in the sopping 90° heat like an iron lid. In the distance, stately oak and sycamore cast patches of shade over green meadow. Along the damper ground, paper-white egrets preen on stick legs. The mood is strangely serene. But it was here, just a few miles east of the silty Mississippi River and the city of St. Louis, that Meyer came to work in the late 1960s with researchers from the University of Wisconsin. And it was here that Cahokia—a ruined capital that once rivaled some Maya city-states in size—commanded the eye.

Meyer sips his water. An art teacher by profession, an artist by preference, the grizzled Illinois native first volunteered his services here as a scientific illustrator: In the months that followed, team members promoted him to field supervisor. They were awash in work. While dissecting one of Cahokia's smaller tumuli, Mound 72, they had stumbled on something unexpected. Entombed beneath a bristling blanket of grass and poison ivy were the rapidly disintegrating bones of hundreds of people. Some had perished naturally at the beginning of the eleventh century; some had died under more suspicious circumstances. But a particularly brutal fate awaited the forty-odd individuals—men and women— in Meyer's sketch.

Indeed, careful studies of physical anthropologists later suggested that all forty spent their last moments lined up along the south end of a 6-foot-deep pit. There executioners had dispatched them one by one, bludgeoning some with a blunt instrument, slicing off the heads of others with something sharper. In the tumult, a few toppled to the bottom alive, their fingers tunneled into the hard clay. As the dust finally settled, bearers arrived, carrying fourteen bodies on wooden litters. Reverently, they arranged the corpses in neat rows on top. Only then, says Meyer, did those responsible cover the grave. "They were doing nasty things to people here," he says finally, eyeing me balefully. "If you have visions of this as being bloodless, that's just ridiculous."

Just what precipitated this slaughter is one of the tantalizing mysteries of North American archaeology, a riddle that researchers are only now beginning to unravel. The most important pre-Columbian capital ever to rise north of the Rio

Grande, Cahokia witnessed more than its share of intrigue and turmoil. Rising near some of the continent's greatest riparian trade routes, not far from where the Illinois and Missouri Rivers flow into the muddy waters of the Mississippi, it spawned ambition. Bordering lands as diverse as the great plains, the eastern woodlands, and the Ozarks, it reaped resources from all. And its fame spread far and wide. At its zenith in the eleventh century, Cahokia boasted an estimated 10,000 to 15,000 inhabitants—a population only slightly smaller than London at that time. Such figures, moreover, do little justice to its might. So revered were its rulers that they commanded the surrounding countryside: Some scholars put populations there as high as another 85,000 people.

All belonged to the Mississippian culture. Masters of the bow and arrow and maize agriculture, Mississippian peoples prospered along river valleys in the Southeast at the beginning of the tenth century. Governed by local chiefs, they founded a string of tiny towns along the broad floodplain adjacent to present-day St. Louis. Cahokia, it seems, was just one of many; but the unprepossessing hamlet was destined for greatness. As the eleventh century unfolded, a new capital emerged like a butterfly from a chrysalis. In the sweltering heat, laborers began leveling ridges and swales for new plazas. They set to work filling baskets with millions of tons of sodden clay and sand for more than 100 mounds. And on distant bluffs, they began hewing and hauling thousands of timbers for mysterious circular monuments. The effect was stunning. Nothing quite like it had ever risen before in the Southeast.

Indeed, scholars are only beginning to appreciate the full extent of these massive public works. Fashioned of wood and earth—materials far more perishable than the stone favored in better-known Maya centers—Cahokia's complex architecture has come to light grudgingly. And as researchers mull over its meaning, they struggle to piece together the intricate prehistory of the capital. How, they ask, did Cahokia rise from obscurity to majesty in just a century? Could some local lord have seized power, rallying the countryside and draping his

Painting of Cahokia. (By L. K. Townsend; courtesy of the Cahokia Mounds State Historic Site.)

hometown in glory? Or did some other force come into play? What purpose did temples, plazas, and monuments serve? And what finally brought Cahokia to its knees in the thirteenth century?

The most intriguing answers have emerged from the research of a brilliant young University of Oklahoma scholar, Tim Pauketat, and just after dawn on an early July morning, I set off across a grassy field at Cahokia Mounds State Historic Site to join him and his crew. In the far distance, cars stream past on a suburban highway, slicing through the heart of the crumbling capital: A police helicopter whirls in the sky above. But here, in this dew-dampened field, an older order prevails. Meadowlarks skim the fescue, singing on the wing. Bees wend drunkenly to the hive. And in every direction, almost as far as the eye can see, small and large grass-covered mounds rise and fall, embossing the land in giant dots and dashes like some huge earthen version of braille.

Indeed, the mind reels at the exorbitance of it all. The huge green hill looming to the north, for example, is none other than Monks Mound. Named after Trappist monks who set up housekeeping at Cahokia briefly in the eighteenth century, the pyramid-shaped ruin swells over some fifteen acres and ascends 100 feet to the sky in stepped terraces—the largest prehistoric edifice ever constructed north of Mexico. The square field adjoining it is the grand plaza, a manufactured plain of some forty acres; the lakes and ponds that shimmer along the edges—one spanning as much as seventeen acres— are pits gouged by workers as they gathered mud for mounds. All conspire to reduce humanity to the stature of ants.

At the far end of the plaza, along a small crest known as Red Mound, Pauketat and his crew unpack their University of Oklahoma van. Already, at six in the morning—the only time of the day when the summer heat and humidity at Cahokia are bearable—crew members buckle down to the work. Rolling back plastic sheets from their shallow pits, they reach for their shovels. Standing in the back of the van, Pauketat surveys the scene. Handing a cooler filled with crew lunches to a student, he shouts advice to a young teaching assistant. "Tell them not to put every morsel through the screen," he says, "it's all redeposited anyway."

Thin and fine-boned, with short, reddish brown hair and a wry manner, the thirty-five-year-old researcher seems re-

Once the preserve of the great lords of Cahokia, Monks Mound still towers over the broad floodplain of the Mississippi River. (Courtesy of the Cahokia Mounds State Historic Site.)

markably relaxed. Dressed for the day in yellow T-shirt, blue cotton pants and green high-topped runners, he looks more like a teenager on holidays than a man trying to complete two complex excavations in torpid heat with a fractious and largely inexperienced crew. With half of his troops here, the other half at a site several miles to the north, he has spent the past week bouncing back and forth like a pinball, cramming down lunches over the steering wheel, shuttling equipment between the sites, and somehow keeping a fragile peace among crew members.

It's an impressive piece of juggling, one that Pauketat pulls off with grace and good humor. But for all his outward calm, he is clearly worried. A month into the field season, he is now two weeks behind schedule. And more delays lie ahead. While clearing off the overburden at the site north of here last week, crew members tumbled upon the corner of a prehistoric cemetery, one that predates the Mississippian inhabitants of Cahokia. Pauketat wants nothing more than to leave the bodies and a ceremonial pot untouched, working around them. But state officials have other ideas. "I'm getting a little pressure to do something with the pot," he concedes, shrugging his shoulders. "Archaeologists hate to leave things like that in case some looter comes back and tries to find it."

Dogged by such bad luck, most researchers would begin paring back their field seasons. Pauketat is sticking to his plans. This is, after all, the work he has long craved. Born just twenty miles from here, Pauketat developed an early fascination for the ancient capital. As a curious child, he often tagged along with his father on deliveries in the region, eager just to gaze on the mounds. A decade later, as a student at the University of Southern Illinois, he embarked on a detailed study of Cahokia. Immersing himself in the minutiae of local ceramics, he soon became an expert on shard tempering and rim-ratio scales, writing his master's thesis on the subject.

Pottery, however, was only a means to an end: His passion was political economy. It soon led to some of his most important work. Keen to see whether commoners in the capital had profited from Cahokia's expansion, the young researcher began casting around for sources of raw data. In years past, many excavators had shelved entire collections after completing digs, never returning to analyze artifacts, features, or maps. "We had more excavations than we really understood," says Pauketat. One collection in particular caught his eye. In the early 1960s, an interstate highway had threatened to chop through Cahokia. To salvage what they could, crews from the Illinois State Museum had peeled away the sod from nearly 100,000 square feet, revealing the outlines of hundreds of houses in an area known as Tract 15A.

As a doctoral student at the University of Michigan at Ann Arbor, Pauketat set to work sifting through the stored contents of these ancient houses. Tabulating each piece of refuse—from pottery shards to chert flakes—he slowly dated the houses with a sensitive new tool of his own devising. In his earlier studies, Pauketat had noticed a certain fickleness among the capital's potters. As migrants poured into Cahokia during the eleventh century, they brought subtle new methods of tempering clay, for example, that were quickly picked up by their neighbors. Intrigued, the young researcher had classified these short-lived trends and dated them by comparison with Cahokian ceramics of known age. While earlier experts could look at pottery fragments from the capital and date them to broad periods of fifty to a hundred years, Pauketat could pin them down to minute subphases averaging just twenty years long.

Such perspicacity soon paid off. Studying the household pottery from 15A carefully, the young researcher succeeded in dating sixty-four homes. And as he grouped these houses—and their domestic refuse—into narrow time periods, he discovered something startling: At the very beginning of the eleventh century, residential districts in Cahokia underwent a radical transformation. "What I got," he says, still marveling over it, "was really more than I looked for. It was a real abrupt change." Long bound to ancestral tradition, the people of Cahokia suddenly abandoned ancient family customs and practices 1,000 years ago: In their place, they embraced the untried, the unproven, the unknown.

Gone, for example, were the traditional neighborhoods. For centuries, families in the region resided in small houses clustered around a central courtyard that served at least on occasion as a private ceremonial ground. As the eleventh century dawned, however, these intimate courtyards vanished from neighborhood plans: Mammoth plazas, capable of holding crowds of thousands, took their place. And families soon discarded traditional methods of house building. Rather than sinking individual holes for each house post, they began carving out long wall trenches for the upright timbers. To Pauketat, it looked suspiciously like the signature of a new kind of house, one that was both thatched and hip-roofed. "And once it appears," he explains, "every single house is wall-trenched after that."

Household contents revealed similar sweeping change. For the first time, residents enjoyed scarce luxury goods—fine imported cherts, copper, lead ore, hematite, basalt, and various mineral crystals. Trade goods were clearly flowing into the capital and someone seemed to be dispensing them liberally. "There's a lot of largesse being given to everyone," says Pauketat. And flint-knappers in the capital were turning out a new triangular style of arrowhead. Finely made from Burlington chert, a stone that naturally assumes shades of blue, these arrowheads had all been carefully heated in fire until they turned a lustrous white. To Pauketat, these beautiful bone-white weapons looked suspiciously like relics of a new warrior cult.

Taken all together, he says, the evidence points in one direction: A great leader had emerged from the shadows. Mastering all rivals, this influential person set a radical new course for the community, persuading one and all to adopt a host of unfamiliar practices. "Someone's in control," Pauketat concludes, bending over to pick up a shovel. "It's my idea that it's like a political takeover. I think there's a series of competing families, and somebody manages to obtain access to resources that formerly were not available and begins sucking it all into the center." While the identity of this great lord will probably never be known, Pauketat believes that the most tantalizing clues were unearthed during the late 1960s from a Cahokian house of the dead.

✦   ✦   ✦

In a quiet, deserted corner of the University of Wisconsin in Milwaukee, Melvin Fowler rustles through the dirt-smudged profiles and dog-eared photographs from Mound 72. A modest man in his early seventies, fond of homespun sayings and self-deprecating humor, Fowler has spent more than a quarter of a century sifting through the voluminous research from his most famous excavation. Retired now from his teaching duties as a professor of anthropology, he spends most weekday mornings at a desk in the archaeology laboratory, thumbing through scientific papers and synthesizing his research into a much awaited final report.

Like other members of the old guard, Fowler first arrived at Cahokia in the early 1960s as highway construction crews were bearing down on the capital. Called in to coordinate the salvage excavations, the conscientious researcher was soon amazed to find that no modern detailed map of the mounds existed. With little recourse but to make his own, Fowler wrangled a grant from the National Science Foundation and began poring over old aerial photographs. Plotting and measuring the locations of all visible tumuli, he noticed something curious. Like other Mississippian peoples, Cahokia's builders constructed most mounds with flat tops. These then served as foundations for chiefly homes and wooden temples, where the bones of revered ancestors and other sacred objects were stored. But some mounds at Cahokia took the shape of ridges or peaked roofs. What purpose did they serve?

Fowler spread out his maps. Four of these ridgetop mounds straddled what appeared to be the capital's central axes. "So we proposed this idea that they were a sort of marker monument." If such were the case, they might reveal both central planning and a powerful civic authority at Cahokia. Curious, Fowler decided to excavate the smallest of these constructions—Mound 72. Noting where the central north-south axis fell, he mustered a small excavation team and began slowly working down into the dank earth. Before long, a crew member hit the walls of a great pit. At the bottom lay a 3-foot-wide circular stain in the soil—the imprint of a giant timber that stood there 1,000 years ago.

Was it an isolated post such as a totem pole or clan marker? Or was it part of something grander? A few years earlier, researchers Warren Wittry and Robert Hall had uncovered remains of a mysterious wooden monument to the west of Monks Mound. Made of tall standing timbers and rebuilt at least four times, Woodhenge formed a circle hundreds of feet wide. Scrutinizing these imprints carefully, Wittry soon theorized that the great timber circle acted as a giant solar calendar much like the better-known Stonehenge. Could the post in Mound 72 mark another Woodhenge?

Fowler expanded the dig. And as he and his crew gently troweled away the earth, they stumbled on something no one expected: the burial of a great lord. On a blanket of some 30,000 shell beads, in a kind of imperial splendor, reclined the skeleton of a man in his forties. Nearby, as if ready to serve him at a moment's notice, stretched six more people—men and women alike—between the ages of seventeen and twenty-one. Tucked around them were a lord's treasures: a long sheet of rolled copper from the Lake Superior region to the north, two bushels of silvery mica imported from North Carolina, piles of smooth stone disks known as chunky stones, and bundles of nearly 1,000 arrows. So identical in size and shape were the arrowheads that they looked as if they had been stamped out by a modern factory.

Fowler was fascinated. Who was this man? The Mississippian people possessed no written language to chronicle the feats of their lords. But perhaps they left some other hint. Fowler pored over the grave goods. During one of his talks at a professional gathering, an audience member noted that the shell blanket formed the outline of a bird. Indeed, with a hooded head and sharp hooked beak, it looked very much like the white silhouette of a falcon or eagle. Fowler was taken aback. "This symbol is very prominent in Mississippian art throughout the Southeast," he says. "In Oklahoma and Georgia, for example, they have these copper plates, and on them are repoussé combinations of humans and falcons."

In historic times, southeastern tribes often depicted one of their deities, the Thunderer, as a falcon. A denizen of the Above World, where true order reigned, the Thunderer was a bird that roosted in the clouds and wrapped itself in lightning. Along the Mississippi River and Great Plains, people had long revered the Thunderer's ability to bring rain, and they feared its fiery force. At times, tribes spoke of the Thunderer and the sun as one—a blurring of lines that is reflected even in this burial. During recent excavations near Mound 72, Fowler has found yet more huge timber imprints, traces of another Woodhenge. And his current calculations suggest that the man on the white-bead blanket rested next to a very particular part of the monument. "That post is the marker post of the summer solstice sunrise," he says.

While mourners and ritualists gradually interred more than 300 other people in this mound, none were accorded such lavish burial as the man on the white-bead blanket. Perhaps, suggests Fowler, they all paid homage to the memory of this great personage. Some, such as the fifty young women discovered side by side in a mass grave, may have played a part in ritual sacrifices; others, interred after natural deaths, may have honored the lord by their sheer presence in the mound. "I would say over a period of a couple of hundred years, this mound was being commemorated just over and over again for the bird man," says Fowler. "Perhaps he was the founding chief of a lineage, and his descendants kept adding to it."

It is even possible, says Pauketat, that he was the lord of Cahokia himself. The exquisitely made arrowheads in his tomb date to the beginning of the eleventh century—the exact period when this great ruler arose. The stockpiles of copper and mica are precisely the kinds of luxuries the lord doled out to loyal followers. And quivers of perfectly made arrows would have greatly befitted a warrior chief who swept to power by cutting down his closest rivals. Indeed, this calculating ruler may even lie near his defeated foes—the forty men and women in Meyer's scrawled sketch. "If you look at other chiefdoms around the world," Pauketat says, "especially Africa, also the Southeast at [the time of European] contact, and South America and Polynesia, typically the enemies were related. There would be a chief and a brother. Or a father and an uncle. So that's why I wonder if the beginning of Cahokia is that kind of event."

+   +   +

On a sultry Saturday afternoon, I bend once again to the shovel, shaving a thin brown curl from the clay at my feet. Quick to snap up an offer of help, Pauketat has put me to work on the far side of Red Mound. After two days of toil, my hands blister; my muscles ache. And as I shovel and toss, shovel and toss, I marvel again at the staggering amount of human labor represented by these mounds. What thoughts ran through the minds of their builders? While some swift act of violence may have swept a great lord to power, says Pauketat, it did not propel construction of these monuments. The secret to all this earthmoving lies somewhere else, it seems—in fervent faith and a sacred tonic known as the Black Drink.

Pauketat first became interested in the subject a few years ago, after reading a paper by colleague Tom Emerson. A former chief archaeologist for the Illinois Historic Preservation Agency and an expert on Mississippian symbolism, Emerson had been studying a distinctive type of decorated pottery found in the region during the late eleventh and early twelfth centuries. Known to archaeologists as Ramey Incised vessels, these pots ranged greatly in size, from small jars to 13-gallon vats. For years, scholars debated their purpose. In his paper, Emerson suggested that early potters turned out these vessels for rituals akin to the secretive Green Corn ceremony.

Among many native tribes of the Southeast, this ritual is the most important religious event of the year. "Essentially," says Pauketat, "it's performed to restore order after the agricultural cycle, to purify people and certain locations and to bring themselves into alignment with supernatural powers."

When European chroniclers first arrived among the Creek, for example, villagers celebrated the ritual just after the corn crop ripened. Local chiefs acted as the sponsors. To prepare for the festival, they commissioned special pots for medicines and mats for certain buildings. Everyone, however, performed some part. As the ceremony began, for example, villagers extinguished their household fires, thus returning the world to the dark chaos that preceded creation. With the first light of dawn, ritualists lit a new fire, bringing life and order to the village again.

In the days that followed, men assembled in the ceremonial grounds: There they received a variety of sacred tonics, some to aid and strengthen them in war, some to purify their bodies. The most notable of these was the Black Drink. Made largely from a native holly, *Ilex cassine* or *Ilex vomitoria*, the Black Drink acted as a potent emetic, inducing vomiting. "It differs somewhat for each group," says Pauketat. "But it's probably intended to purge your body, and then there's a feast to greet the new corn."

Had the lords of Cahokia once presided over similar ceremonies? Had they commissioned Ramey pots for this purpose? Pauketat began gathering clues. From his earlier ceramic studies, he could see that the Ramey pots unearthed in 15A all possessed much the same types of tempers in much the same proportions. Potters scattered throughout the region were unlikely to follow such a pat recipe. All these pots came from one place. But was it Cahokia? Digging through the scientific literature, Pauketat noticed that excavators found the largest Ramey pots in the capital. As they moved farther away into the countryside, they found smaller and smaller vessels: Twelve miles from the capital, Ramey pots measured just half the size of those recovered in Cahokia. Clearly, the largest pots remained exactly where they were made: They were too heavy and fragile to survive a long journey.

After studying the evidence, Pauketat is convinced that Cahokia potters turned out these jars for rituals such as the Green Corn ceremony. And he believes that the great lord sponsoring these events wished to impart a message to celebrants. Along the rims of the Ramey jars, potters incised patterns rich in symbolism. Some match the spirals, sunbursts, and other circular designs closely associated in traditional southeastern belief with the sun and sacred fire. Others resemble falcon tails or stylized weeping eyes. "If you look at a falcon, you'll see these white feathers that come down in a weeping-eye design," notes Pauketat. "In the Southeast you have falcon dancers that have that on them. So it seems pretty secure that that's a falcon symbol." Indeed, the entire rim resembled a metaphor for the Above World, where divine order prevailed.

To Pauketat, such sanctioned symbols strongly suggest that the lords of Cahokia ruled by strength of religion. Persuasive, charismatic, and forceful, they seem to have convinced followers of their ability to intercede with deities of the Above World, ensuring the fertility of the earth, the abundance of the harvest, and the health of all. Indeed, in the eyes of commoners, these lords may well have become divinities themselves. So revered were they that they attracted throngs of people from the countryside during ceremonial events—hence the need for great plazas. "The size of the grand plaza at Cahokia, that's another signature of how many people, how big a festival they might have had there," Pauketat says. "That's likely where they were held."

Such ceremonies, moreover, may have given rise to mounds. To prepare for the Green Corn festival, for example, Creek warriors sprinkled handfuls of clean sand over the ceremonial grounds. At Cahokia, many of the tumuli reveal traces of similar annual rites. When a team of researchers cut through the Kunneman Mound in the 1950s, for example, they found dozens of minute laminations of soil and sand—thirty-three in the lower third of the mound. Sandwiched between many were the fragmentary remains of temples and chiefly houses. "So it's not just the mound," says Pauketat. "They're also redoing the building on top. And that's a lot of labor."

In all likelihood, commoners from across the countryside labored together on the mounds, purifying them with new layers of clean earth for the annual ceremonies. "It's a debt they owe someone, perhaps for ritual services or for the chief being the chief. They owe that person something because that person is mediating the order of the universe and keeping things right for them."

✦ ✦ ✦

In the sixteenth century, a Spanish adventurer with a heart of tempered steel led a small army on a brutal three-year-long trek through the American Southeast. A member of the Spanish force that had trampled the Inka empire in Peru, Hernando de Soto had developed a taste for the life of a conqueror. Catching word of wealth in a huge undefined region the Spanish called Florida, he wrested permission from the Spanish crown to conquer these fabled lands. Wandering the American Southeast in search of plunder, de Soto soon came face-to-face with mound-building peoples—members of the still-enduring Mississippian culture.

Devoted as de Soto and his followers were to tracking down wealth, they soon noticed a striking pattern. "From a distance," noted one chronicler, "the habitations of the lord appeared because they were situated in the highest place, and they revealed themselves to be his by a size and construction superior to the others" (Pauketat 1993). Adorned with finely woven mats, the rulers' homes were invariably sumptuous and spacious and perched on mounds high above the homes of their followers.

On a sultry July evening, I think of this description as I clamber up the steep wooden steps of Monks Mound. The highest point of land for miles, the great mound towers over the floodplain. Reaching the summit, I stroll along its grassy expanse, watching a flock of birds veer gracefully past at eye level. Along the broad plain below, cars whip along the ribbon of highway, speeding into the distance. Suburban trailer courts and ramshackle apartments, discount appliance stores and butcher shops huddle against the edges of far mounds, giving off a sad air of neglect and quiet desperation.

Some 800 years ago, however, this mound was the preserve of the lords of Cahokia. And from this vantage point, on a warm summer night like this, they commanded a stunning view of their realm. To the north, along a winding creek, men pulled dugout canoes ashore, picking out the day's catch of catfish and drum. Hunters threaded past thatched houses, bows slung over their shoulders and a brace of ducks in their hands. In shadowed doorways, older men flaked tools and gossiped contentedly, while young women nursed their infants. Inside, pots of corn and fish stews simmered on the open hearths.

In their elaborate homes atop the smaller mounds, the lesser chiefs entertained kin from the outlying communities. Graciously receiving their guests' gifts of salt, fine imported chert, and other luxuries, they laid out great bowls filled with the finest cuts of deer meat and thin corn breads. Below, in a plaza to the east, a spirited crowd gathered around a game of chunky, a sport still played centuries later when Europeans arrived in the Southeast. As the crowd traded jokes, two nobles and their followers wagered recklessly on the outcome of a match. Picking up the disklike chunky stone, one of the players weighed it in his hand, then smoothly tossed it along the hard-packed clay. A second later, two spears arched into the air, their hard flint edging as close as possible to the final destination of the stone.

Such peaceful summer evenings must have brought a sense of contentment, an illusion that all was forever right with the world. But the secret ambitions of lesser chiefs, the dreams of grandeur and divine power, were not easily harnessed. Those who reigned over Cahokia had need of diplomacy and cunning and the ability to read human hearts. Not every generation produced such a person. By the beginning of the twelfth century, just 100 years or so after the rise of the first great Cahokian lord, chaos began to raise its serpent head in the quiet capital.

Just who launched the threat is not clear. But all at once, work parties began tearing down the houses of commoners in the central precinct of Cahokia. Hauling in 20,000 timbers from the surrounding bluffs, they begin erecting an immense stockade around the central mounds and the great plaza. With bastions spaced every 65 feet or so—about the effective range of a Cahokian archer—the stockade was clearly designed to keep attackers out. And it was soon put to a stern test. Dozens of arrowheads with distinctive impact fractures littered the soil nearby. "It's not a question of invaders coming from afar," says Pauketat. "It's probably a question of local Mississippian politics." Perhaps it was some ruthless younger son, or an ambitious brother. But whoever lay behind it put Cahokia's lords on the defensive.

To the west of Monks Mound, ancient work parties labored feverishly on a series of large private compounds, each defended with bastions. Plastered with a distinctive orange-colored clay, these private quarters may once have acted as secret ritual grounds. But Pauketat now wonders if they could have been put to a far different purpose—guarding the vast stores of corn and other wealth amassed by the lord and his faithful nobles. "There's more and more emphasis on emerging class differences," he says, "and less on keeping everyone integrated as a cohesive social body."

Certainly, it was during this critical period that people began spilling out from the capital like water from a cracked pot. Packing up floor mats and water jars, storage bags and clothing, families abandoned their thatched houses. Tired of dissent perhaps, no longer persuaded that the chiefs of Cahokia communed with the gods, they set out into the countryside. Undoubtedly, some made their way south. Along the silty banks of the great river and its tributaries, a series of Mississippian centers, each with temple mounds and chiefs, rose and fell over the succeeding centuries.

But others, with family ties to the north and west, may well have journeyed to the edges of the Great Plains. In the thirteenth century, says Pauketat, the ancestors of the Osage, Ponca, Omaha, and Winnebago peoples migrated west from a region surrounding the confluence of the Ohio and Mississippi Rivers, and tantalizing fragments of evidence link them to Cahokia. The Osage language, for example, is replete with words for religion and rank—just as one might expect from the devout, class-conscious citizenry of Cahokia. And among the Winnebago, chiefs were always drawn from the Thunderbird clan, part of a larger group known as Those Who Are Above.

But Cahokia itself was forgotten. The timbers of its palisades creaked in the wind and tumbled. Its once great temples and chiefly homes moldered in the ground. Prairie grasses slowly took seed in the flanks of the mounds. By the beginning of the fourteenth century, the fertile lands along this stretch of the Mississippi River were abandoned, a mysterious vacant quarter. The great lord had gone.

8

KILLING FIELDS
Head-Smashed-In Buffalo Jump, Alberta

Skill is stronger than strength.

—W. G. BENHAM

Beneath a weathered rim of sandy gray cliff in the Porcupine Hills of southwestern Alberta, a small team of young cocksure archaeologists set to work in the summer of 1965, peeling back the faded green sod. Perched on an upper slope of bleached prairie, along the far western edges of the Great Plains, Brian Reeves and his associates burrowed down into the dark earth, levering loose a layer of sandstone rubble, the scattered debris from a turn-of-the-century quarry. In the rusty-orange soil below, they spotted the first signs of strange treasure: fragments of rotting bison hide embedded with dozens of small arrowheads. Reeves and his crew were elated. Beneath their hands and feet lay a vast, unplumbed boneyard—the last remains of a legendary buffalo jump, Head-Smashed-In.

In previous decades, discoveries of delicate stone arrowheads beneath this cliff had attracted scientists from as far afield as the American Museum of Natural History in New York and the University of New Mexico in Albuquerque. But little was known about these excavations, for the findings had never been published. As summer lengthened, Reeves, then a graduate student at the University of Calgary, and his crew burrowed deeper and deeper into the earth. The state of preservation was haunting. In one layer of sediment, team members pried loose bison skeletons with still identifiable hair, hide, entrails—even feces. They were 700 years old.

Team members bent back to their work. Some 16 feet beneath the surface, Reeves reduced the yawning pit to a narrow vertical shaft, a structure more characteristic of excavation in ancient Middle Eastern cities than in transient North American campsites. He hammered together a makeshift crane to haul out buckets of soil. In the blistering summer heat, surrounded by towering walls of decomposing bison carcasses, crew members fell mysteriously ill from some strange viral infection. Still, they continued. At last, at a depth of 30 feet, after gingerly exhuming butchered bison bones dating back 5,700 years, Reeves and his colleagues slammed into bedrock.

It seemed like rock bottom, and Reeves and his crew agreed to pack it in, relieved to be done with the dank, cramped pit. But a year later, when Geological Survey of Canada scientist Archibald Stalker arrived with a dragline to study the geology of Head-Smashed-In, evidence of yet another, deeper bone bed emerged. In the soil washing out from beneath a massive block of sandstone that had slumped from the cliff more than 5,700 years ago, Reeves and Stalker fished out pieces of butchered bison bone and a few crude stone choppers. Today, despite renewed excavations by researchers from the University of Calgary, nobody really knows how deep or how ancient the bone beds at Head-Smashed-In really are.

But that is only one mystery now baffling archaeologists. In recent years, the lichen-covered cliff located 100 miles south of Calgary has come under intense scientific scrutiny—with perplexing results. The most complex and best preserved of more than 100 prehistoric bison jumps sprinkled across the North American plains, Head-Smashed-In remains one of the most cunning traps and brilliant ruses ever devised by prehistoric humans in pursuit of big game. Over the past 5,700 years, native hunters outwitted more than 123,000 of North

The cliff at the Head-Smashed-In Buffalo Jump. Without horses or rifles, hunters once maneuvered great herds of bison over this precipice. (By Jack Brink; courtesy of the Provincial Museum of Alberta.)

America's largest terrestrial animals along the grassy slopes west of the jump, luring them to their death. "Head-Smashed-In is a monument to native people," says Reeves, a professor of archaeology in Calgary. "It's a monument to the achievement of a culture that is unparalleled in all prehistory."

And yet after countless hours of scientific investigation and analysis, researchers are only now beginning to grasp how the ingenious system worked. The greatest puzzle is how the bison herds were gathered and controlled. Although European traders and explorers penned eyewitness accounts of other northern plains bison jumps in the early 1800s, most focused on the final bloody spectacle of bison hurtling over precipitous cliffs. All described bands of hunters that possessed horses. But North American native tribes did not become equestrians until the Spanish brought horses to the New World in the 1500s. Before then, they traveled on foot. So how, wonder archaeologists, did pedestrian bands round up bison in the sprawling grasslands west of Head-Smashed-In and drive them with pinpoint accuracy to a predetermined spot? Bison have been clocked at speeds of up to 30 miles per hour, and as American plains archaeologist and former bison rancher George Frison once wrote, the shaggy beast seems "to move awkwardly and think slowly, but a few minutes in a corral with one will rapidly dispel this kind of thinking" (Frison 1978).

Moreover, in an era long before refrigeration or canning, what became of the vast stores of meat produced at Head-Smashed-In? In one drive alone, ancient band members slaughtered 225 of the beasts, amassing a mountain of 100,000 pounds of meat. Could hunters there have devised some means of preserving their kill? And could these vast stores of meat have become the foundation of an intricate transcontinental trade, linking plains hunters to the wealthy chiefs of Mississippian farming communities?

"The more I study, the more I get boggled at how they pulled these things off," says Jack Brink on a sizzling late-April afternoon as he leads the way up the path below the ancient jump. A tall, angular man in his early forties, with hay-colored hair and the easy plainspoken manner of a prairie wheat farmer, Brink is head of the Archaeological Survey at The Provincial Museum of Alberta. Drawing to a stop finally beneath a craggy sandstone cliff that towers some 30 feet into the air, he turns the visor of a sweat-stained baseball cap to shade the back of his neck. Satisfied, he glances up at the lethal rim of Head-Smashed-In. Named by the neighboring Piikáni tribe in remembrance of a curious boy who died as he hid under the cliff to watch a jump from below, Head-Smashed-In gives little evidence today of its thunderous past. In the morning light, marmots sun along the high crannies; a pair of cliff swallows fuss over a nest along an overhang. Butterflies wobble over the grasses below.

A stubborn, forthright man with an abiding interest in bison jumps, Brink has been studying Head-Smashed-In for more than a decade. But unlike many earlier researchers, who gravitated naturally enough to the bone bed and its rich lode of arrowheads, Brink has long been fascinated by the fields behind the jump. "As I got into the literature and into the handling of bison and the manipulations," he explains, "I started to realize that there's no pile of bones unless the other parts of the operation work. The key to it all is back in some other direction, miles away from where the bones lie now."

To illustrate his point, he takes me out the next morning in a dusty sedan, following Spring Point Road around the southern end of the Porcupine Hills. Just beyond lies the grassy reservation lands of the north Piikáni (or north Peigan as the Europeans called them), members of the Blackfoot Nation that once ranged the prairies of southern Alberta and northern Montana. Along the horizon to the west rise the whitened peaks of the Rocky Mountains, shimmering like specters. But we swing north this morning, heading toward the country west of Head-Smashed-In. Rimmed on three sides with a rugged highland and threaded by small finger basins and gullies, this green basin is favored grazing land even today; as Brink and I hop out of the car and set off on foot up a ridge, dozens of sturdy cattle eye us suspiciously.

Partway up the slope, Brink points out a small, scarcely noticeable cluster of seven or eight stones. As I soon see, identical heaps fleck the ground every four or five paces, forming a giant dotted line along the crest of land. The cairns, Brink explains, border both sides of a long, low-lying channel, a natural route for driving bison from the southwest toward the jump. Similar mounds have been recorded at many other northern plains jumps, but until recently, few archaeologists paid them much mind. "Almost everyone mentioned whether they were there or not," says Brink, "these small rock piles leading to the jump, but hardly anyone gave one iota of thought, as far as I can tell, to how they worked."

Indeed, most researchers simply assumed that hazers once crouched behind the cairns, concealing themselves until they darted out at the last minute to frighten the herds on toward the jump. But such a scenario was difficult to imagine at Head-Smashed-In, where flat clusters of rock sprinkled the prairie. What was going on? Perhaps, suggested Brink, herds of cattle had trampled the original cairns. Or perhaps wind-blown soil had buried the high cairns, leaving only the crest

Stone cairns that line the drive lanes at Head-Smashed-In. Topped with brush and strips of rawhide, these rock piles helped funnel bison into a lethal trap. (By Jack Brink; courtesy of the Provincial Museum of Alberta.)

exposed. Both theories seemed plausible. But excavations conducted by graduate student Maureen Rollans in the mid-1980s revealed no such destruction.

Puzzled, Brink began to see other holes in the conventional theory. Until late prehistoric times, the northern plains had been sparsely populated by small, widely scattered bands. It seemed unlikely that leaders of the hunts could ever have marshaled a workforce of 1,000 people. But at Head-Smashed-In, one drive lane skipped for more than four miles along the rolling grasslands and contained an estimated 1,200 cairns. "You couldn't ever have had nearly enough hunters to put people behind all of them," notes Brink. "So it seems inescapable to me that these things somehow had an immediate, direct function to move bison and to do it by themselves, without hunters stationed behind them."

But how could obscure stone clusters move a herd? Turning to early historic accounts of bison jumps, Brink noticed references to piles of brush bordering the drive lanes. "Some of the early explorers called these things 'dead men,' and it's never made clear why." Surveyors today use the term to describe anchoring points, but Brink wondered whether those in historic times used the term more literally. It is quite possible, he now argues, that the hunters built them to take the place of a human being. "They wanted something that showed motion. If you can do that without having a hunter there, then you can concentrate your people at the end of the jump, where you really need them."

Band members, he now suggests, could easily have wedged a piece of brush into the center of each rock cluster and tied long strips of rawhide to the branches. In the wind, these pieces of hide would wriggle and snap in the air, creating a row of swaying, teetering scarecrows. And as a herd of bison passed through a pair of these drive lines, says Brink, it would glimpse movement on the ridges and remain warily on the downside. Such a deception, capitalizing cleverly on their prey's limited vision, permitted hunters to deploy their forces to better purpose.

Still, much remained a mystery. While puzzling over the cairns, Brink and others realized they needed a more complete map of the lines. An early attempt to chart them by remote-sensing techniques had failed. So Brink asked Reeves to return and map as many as possible in the grasslands behind Head-Smashed-In. The results astounded everyone. During his methodical rambles, Reeves recorded an intricate labyrinth of more than thirty intersecting drive lines, containing an estimated 12,000 to 20,000 cairns.

Across the Great Plains, archaeologists had never recorded such a complex system before; most other jumps relied on simple pairs of drive lines that funneled herds toward a cliff. But what puzzled Reeves and Brink most was the bizarre locations of many lines. Some led away from Head-Smashed-In to high, remote buttes, while others seemed to converge on small cliffs circling the northern perimeter of the basin. "The whole thing was just completely turned around and different from what we had expected," says Reeves. "There were many locales they were directing bison towards, only one of which was Head-Smashed-In."

Were some of these northern cliffs bison jumps as well? Curious now, Brink and Reeves set out to take a look. While wandering the bleached grasses below one lethal-looking cliff, they found scraps of bone. Laying out a series of pits there, colleague Susan Marshall and a small crew soon exhumed yellowing bison bone from at least four separate hunts. Perched along the cliffs less than a mile north of Head-Smashed-In, the Calderwood Jump seems to have served as an alternative kill site when the wind was blowing unfavorably for running bison to the south.

But no one knows whether hunters were driving herds off the other northern cliffs. Although field crews have walked their bases, they have turned up little clear sign of bone beds. Even so, both Reeves and Brink now speculate that the lines once led to a network of lethal jumps in the southern Porcupine Hills, an elaborate system that permitted hunters to control and move herds at will. "They could use an interrelated set of lanes—depending on which finger basin they were in and which way the wind was blowing—to bring the bison toward one of the series of jumps," says Reeves. "There may be as many as six or seven more buffalo jumps around the north perimeter of the basin." While Head-Smashed-In remained the jump of choice, the deadliest part of the system, hunters likely made use of many other cliffs when the winds shifted slightly. In this rolling, broken country they were never at a loss.

More and more, the peaceful, sun-bleached grasslands here are beginning to look like a vast killing field.

✦   ✦   ✦

In a tidy, sunlit kitchen, Billy Strikes With A Gun summons up memory of an ancient mystery. An animated, expressive man, with cropped ash-gray hair and a friendly manner, Strikes With A Gun speaks slowly in his native Blackfoot, rapping the table lightly from time to time with his hand. "The drive lanes, the jump, it was all magic to the buffalo," he says through friend and interpreter Reg Crowshoe. "They couldn't understand what was happening. If their leader went over, they all went over. And if they survived something like that, the magic of the buffalo stone wiped it out of their minds."

Until settling down just over a century ago to reservation life, the Piikáni were expert bison hunters, the last people to use Head-Smashed-In before it was abandoned around 1860. Now in his eighties, a respected elder of the tribe, Strikes With A Gun still cherishes the stories he heard as a small child of how his relatives and other members of the Blackfoot Nation once lured great herds to their deaths. For Strikes With A Gun and many others on this reservation, the days of bison hunting are far from forgotten.

This morning, sitting in a kitchen filled with mementos—black-and-white photographs of medicine men in traditional buckskin, canisters brimming with brightly colored beads for beadwork—Strikes With A Gun recalls tales of the buffalo stone or *iniskim*. A small fossil shaped by nature like a miniature bison and rubbed smooth with red ocher, the stone once played a key part in the hunt. It was this sacred charm, explains the elder, that gave his people their power over the shaggy beasts. All night before a drive, ritualists gathered together to perform ceremonies with the *iniskim*, enticing bison to the jump. Then, just before dawn, they summoned the buffalo runners—young, unmarried men of great endurance and speed.

Preparing themselves for the ordeal ahead, the runners donned the skins of antelope, the fastest animals known to the Blackfoot, and the hides of buffalo; some chewed autzkwiksi root to increase their speed. After prayers and a blessing, they set out under a starry sky. Heading away from the cliff's edge, they loped along ridges of the basin behind, looking for a herd of cows and calves. In such a sprawling grassland, says Brink, "it's hard to imagine that there might not ever be any." Two or three days might pass in the search, but when a large herd was finally spotted, the runners would wait patiently until the small hours of the morning before leading the bison in the direction of a jump.

To drive the wary animals, a runner in antelope skins might bound in and out of the bisons' range of vision, skillfully changing the direction of the herd; another runner, dressed in bison hide and headdress, might mimic the distinctive bleating of a panic-stricken calf, luring the worried herd forward. Observers found the runners' talents uncanny. "Their gestures so closely resembled those of the animals themselves that had I not been in on the secret, I should have been as much deceived as the oxen," wrote fur trader Alexander Henry of runners from the Assiniboine tribe (Verbicky-Todd 1984).

Keeping constant watch on wind direction, never allowing the animals to pick up human scent, the runners guided the herd into a chosen set of drive lines. Along the basin rim, sentries tracked their progress, alerting the main camp to the herd's approach. There band members, men and women alike, hastened to their posts along the end of the route. Many offered up prayers. As the runners led the powerful animals toward them, the herd bunched tighter and tighter in the subtly converging drive lines. At last, sensing danger, the cows broke into a stampede.

Leading the pounding animals down the final stretch, the swiftest runner panted, fearful of being trodden underfoot. There was no room for error. If the runner failed to leap out of the herd's path in time, he would be swept over the precipice in the tide of animals. And other band members held their breath, too. At any moment, the lead cow might swerve out of the lane, trampling all hazers in her path. "The stories I heard from my grandmothers," says Strikes With A Gun, "they were scared the way the buffalo looked. They were all ready to run away from the drive lanes, but they couldn't leave. They had to stay at their posts. The buffalo all came down the lanes, their heads down, full charge, all mad and looking mean."

But the odds were stacked against the terrified animals. On the final dash to Head-Smashed-In, the lane angled gently downward, increasing the fatal momentum of the top-heavy bison and making veering or stopping all but impossible. Few animals could see what lay ahead, surrounded as they were by a cloud of dust and churning bodies. Even the lead cow could not have been certain until the last lethal moment, for prairie ran up to the cliff edge, creating an alluring optical illusion— a continuous grassy carpet that seemed to stretch to the eastern horizon. As the panicking animals raced headlong toward the fatal trap, the sun rose over the brow of prairie, momentarily blinding them. There was no way out. Dazzled, confused, and enchanted, they thundered over the edge, where knots of hunters waited below.

✦ ✦ ✦

During the closing years of the eighteenth century, a young English fur trader wintered with Piikáni hunters in the foothills of the Rocky Mountains. An impressionable man of twenty-three, Peter Fidler was one of the few Europeans ever to witness and record the Piikáni at their lethal work in trade. For the young Englishman, not yet accustomed to the hard life of the northern plains, the final slaughter of an entire herd of the great shaggy animals was a sight not soon forgotten. "The Hatchet is frequently used," he reported, "and it is shocking to see the poor animals thus pent up without any way of escaping, butchered in this shocking manner . . ." (Verbicky-Todd 1984).

But the Piikáni had no such reservations. To young and old alike, such drives were known as *pis'kun*, "deep kettle of blood," and they soon set to work butchering their prey for a great feast. The ground flowed with dark blood. But while Fidler and other Europeans marveled at such scenes and the success of the Piikáni and other plains bison hunters, they paid little attention to what became of all the amassed meat. To modern researchers such as Brink, it has become a point of contention. What did small bands of plains hunters do with all the slaughtered game?

Curious, Brink decided to take a closer look, excavating a broad bench of prairie beneath the jump. Situated a short stroll downhill and downwind from the slaughtering grounds, this bench seemed tailor-made for butchering carcasses. But the dig soon turned into a frustrating game of patience. For thousands of years, hunters had trampled their refuse into a dense pavement of bone and rock that stubbornly resisted excavation. "It's like someone ran over a book with a bulldozer, and all we've got is one page," says Brink. Nevertheless, he and his crews persisted over nine field seasons. In the end, they pieced together a fascinating chronicle of prehistoric life.

Among nearly 1,000 arrowheads and dart points that team members recovered from the broad bench of prairie, only a handful belonged to the earliest cultures at Head-Smashed-In. In Brink's view, these bands likely butchered their prey right where it fell beneath the cliff and then consumed only the choice cuts. "They left what in later times would be regarded as an awful lot of food value," he notes. "These people weren't concerned with storage of food or with getting all the nutritional value out of a carcass that they possibly could. It was more like, 'Let's get a big meat meal; let's stuff ourselves and get out of here.' "

But 2,000 years ago, hunters took a radically different approach. Like bison hunters across the northern plains, they began painstakingly processing their kill. After drying or roasting the bison flesh on hearths, they crushed the animals' long bones into splinters, boiling fragments to make bone grease. The work was hard and tedious. To boil bones, band members first heated stones in a fire, then dropped them into a hide-lined pit filled with water. And the labor did not stop there. Good boiling stones were rare at Head-Smashed-In: The local sandstone absorbed too much water and crumbled during heating. To obtain better rock, families hauled in tons of quartzite, limestone, and granite from sites more than a mile away. "They went to a considerable amount of effort to get this," marvels Brink, "and it's got to be one of the hardest things to carry in all of prehistoric life. It's not like carrying hides or meat or tepee poles, all which you can drag, haul, or drape over yourself."

But to what purpose? Reading through the historic literature, Brink noticed that the Piikáni and other bison hunters had once rendered bone grease to mix with smashed dried meat and saskatoon berries. The result was pemmican—"one of the most effective methods of food processing ever devised," wrote American scholar Tom McHugh (Verbicky-Todd 1984). Not only did the grease add to usable protein in the meat, it also sealed the mixture from airborne moisture, preserving it for decades. According to some accounts, a bag of well-made pemmican could be safely consumed twenty years after it had been prepared.

In all likelihood, says Brink, hunters at Head-Smashed-In turned out their first rawhide bags of pemmican some 2,000 years ago. And chances are that this new, highly storable food soon became a highly valuable commodity. "Perhaps the people [at Head-Smashed-In] were overproducing for the sake of trade," says Brink, "and in fact killing bison way beyond what they needed, killing bison to produce a large surplus that they would then send out elsewhere. They may well have become essentially dealers in bison products." Brimming with protein—three to five times the nourishment of fresh meat, in fact—lightweight pemmican made a superb backpacking food. And such nutritious trail food would have been highly welcome among the wealthy traders in settlements along the Mississippi River, some 1,500 miles to the southeast. "You could trade pemmican and hides a considerable distance," says Brink. "Why not Cahokia?"

Just how the pemmican trade may have worked and just what easterners—and their intermediaries—offered in exchange for the protein-rich fare remain unclear. Brink suggests that the Mississippian peoples may have traded goods such as corn or tobacco, commodities whose traces may well have escaped the eyes of excavators. But it's also possible that plains traders received far less tangible goods from time to time, returning home from their journeys east with marriage partners, songs, dances, and rituals—perhaps even some of the oldest rites of the Sun Dance.

✦   ✦   ✦

In an airy sunlit living room in Calgary, Brian Reeves leans back and sips a cup of freshly brewed cappuccino. A thin, owlish man with a scholarly and personal knowledge of the old west that is little short of astonishing, Reeves has spent the last hour or so discoursing on the truths conveyed in oral history. Sitting on a couch, within easy reach of a telephone that rings constantly, Reeves considers the origins of the Sun Dance, the most famous and sacred of all rituals on the northern plains.

Held at the height of summer, the Sun Dance, or Medicine Lodge as the Piikáni prefer to call it, has long captured the imagination of outsiders. A mainstay of traditional plains life, the Sun Dance spans several days and centers upon prayers for the fertility of all living things and the health of all tribal members. By far the best-known part of the ceremony, however, is the piercing ritual. To fulfill sacred vows, tribal members step forward to have their chest and back muscles skewered with sharpened bones. Ritualists then tie ropes that drape down from the Sun Dance Lodge's center pole to these skewers. To complete the ceremony, the sun dancers swing back and forth against the ropes until their flesh tears free.

From the journals of early Europeans in the region, it is clear that the Piikáni and their neighbors have performed the Sun Dance for more than a century. But the origins of the ritual, says Reeves, go back to a much more distant time and to a legendary figure known to the Piikáni as Scarface. Sadly disfigured and orphaned as a young boy, Scarface was said to have fallen in love with a particularly beautiful young woman. But she refused to marry someone so deformed. Unable to put her out of his mind, the young man climbed the Sweetgrass Hills to pray. There a spirit appeared, bringing news that he could be cured by the sun. Encouraged, the boy set out on a long journey over prairies, rivers, mountains, and a great body of water to the sun's lodge. After many trials, he succeeded in winning the sun's favor. His face was healed. As a final parting gift, the great divinity taught him the secrets of the Medicine Lodge to take back to his people. In memory of Scarface, the Piikáni long held the ceremony in the Sweet-grass Hills.

Leaning back in his chair, Reeves explains that such sacred stories are often grounded in historical fact. Legends concerning the origins of the buffalo stone, for example, describe a place called Falling-Off-Without-Excuse: By carefully following clues in the story, Reeves has recently discovered the site—a place where the particular fossil favored for buffalo stones abounds. And the careful researcher is now convinced that much truth underlies the stories of the origins of the Medicine Lodge. Indeed, he believes that the Scarface of the myth may well have been someone involved in the Mississippian trade.

Four years ago, says Reeves, a southern Alberta art teacher and his three brothers took shelter from a severe summer hailstorm in a small cave in the Sweetgrass Hills. As the four men waited out the storm, they noticed a number of arrowheads poking out from the soft soil. Curious, they began digging. A foot and a half beneath the ground, one of the campers pulled out what he thought at first was a bicycle seat. It was an ancient gorget—a throat ornament—made of a large seashell. Burrowing deeper, they soon found another. Carved from shimmering white shell, the gorgets were identical to those interred with Mississippian nobles and priests. "They're probably about a thousand years old," says Reeves.

Realizing they had stumbled on something important, the four men quit digging and reported the find to authorities. And there matters rest today. Archaeologists have yet to excavate the site, and federal authorities are now attempting to determine who has legal ownership of the gorgets—the southern Piikáni, in whose traditional territory they were found, or the Creek tribe, descendants of the Mississippian people. But Reeves now believes that the cave holds the body of a historical personage very important to the Piikáni. "That might be the burial of some Mississippian person in there who was a high-status male, a priest, a merchant or whatever, who could be connected with the bringing of the Medicine Lodge."

The Sweetgrass Hills, after all, overlook the Milk River—a tributary of the Missouri River that flows into the Mississippi and past Cahokia. And much research suggests that the Mississippian people greatly revered the sun as a deity. Studies have shown, for example, that the circular wooden monuments known as Woodhenge at Cahokia were closely tied to celebrations of key solar events such as the solstice. Indeed one scholar, Robert Hall, now suggests that Woodhenge may have served as a world center shrine, gathering in the potent blessings of the sun for the benefit of the community. This, too, is the purpose of the Medicine Lodge, a large, circular, wooden structure.

Could an ancient Piikáni trader returning from the east have brought some of the Mississippian religion with him, giving rise to the Sun Dance? Reeves, for one, thinks it's eminently possible. "It's the most logical source for it. And it's the kind of thing that would spread very fast along the northern plains, among buffalo hunting people. Each in its own form."

✦   ✦   ✦

But as Reeves and others puzzle over evidence of time-honored legends and transcontinental trade at Head-Smashed-In, others such as Thomas Kehoe seek clues to even more ancient mysteries. A veteran plains archaeologist now retired from his post as curator of anthropology at the Milwaukee Public Museum, Kehoe believes that the early hunters at Head-Smashed-In offer a crucial key to a culture that lived an ocean away and more than 10,000 years earlier.

Kehoe, a small, sprightly man who spent seven years living among the southern Piikáni in Montana and later served as Saskatchewan's first provincial archaeologist, has had a career-long fascination with big-game-hunting cultures. In the late 1960s, this interest led him to central France, where archaeologists had found 17,000-year-old butchered horse bones beneath a prominent local cliff known as the Rock of

Solutré. As the excavations there proceeded, researchers turned up the remains of at least 10,000 horses, suggesting that Upper Paleolithic hunters in the region were communally driving the herds over a jump.

Solutré whetted Kehoe's curiosity. In 1978, he returned to Europe, and during spring break from his teaching post at the University of Tübingen, in Germany, he shepherded a group of students through southern Europe's cave-art sites. On arriving at the most famous of these, the French site of Lascaux, with its naturalistic murals of stampeding game painted nearly 17,000 years ago, Kehoe was dumbfounded. "Almost immediately, I was greeted by a familiar sight. What I recognized when I first saw the primitive diagram on the wall was a depiction of an animal drive in the manner of the Blackfeet Indians."

At the center of the large diagram, situated on the south wall of the Axial Gallery, was a painted rectangle, with one line of dots emanating from its lower right corner and another from its lower left. To an archaeologist who had excavated bison jumps in Montana and listened to stories of Piikáni elders, the fan-shaped dotted lines looked suspiciously like rock clusters leading to a trap—a rectangular corral. "In front of the corral, there's a little black horse just about to enter," says Kehoe, "and way back down the way, there's the head and shoulders of another black horse that's running up. Then farther down, there's a whole herd being driven up through."

Studying the south wall more closely, Kehoe discerned paintings of reindeer, wild oxen, and wild goats skidding into four other corrals. On the opposite wall, the painters had depicted two horses, one attempting to halt before a precipice, the other tumbling helplessly head over heels off the edge. The more Kehoe looked around, the more he felt at home. Even a controversial two-horned figure known as the Unicorn struck a familiar chord. "It looked more like a man in some sort of camouflage," explains Kehoe. "I think he is the runner bringing them in."

Kehoe's observations, delivered at an international congress on zooarchaeology in Bordeaux, France, set European researchers astir. Since the discovery of the beautifully limned panels, scholars have struggled to decipher their meaning. While some viewed them simply as art for art's sake, others saw deeper meaning, interpreting them as representations of shamanism, symbols of fertility, and emblems of totemism. But Kehoe, with his extensive knowledge of animal behavior and New World bison-hunting cultures, is convinced they record adrenaline-charged scenes of 17,000-year-old animal drives.

Moreover, in Kehoe's carefully considered view, the communal hunting techniques depicted at Lascaux and at other European cave-art sites mark an important milestone in human evolution. The jumps, traps, and corrals that the painters portray were "extremely important in the making of man because you have a new method of hunting, a new mechanism," he explains. "It's no longer one man or two or three men on one animal; it's a group of people being able to hunt a whole herd at one time." And such newfound collaboration could have far-reaching consequences. "When you have a larger group of people getting together, you expand the gene pool," says Kehoe, "and that means you have changes."

Kehoe now believes that communal hunting may have started as early as the very dawn of the Upper Paleolithic era, some 40,000 years ago. At the time, Neanderthal bands were beginning to vanish from their European homelands, only to be replaced by their closest kin, *Homo sapiens sapiens*. "Maybe Neanderthals could have been involved [in communal hunting] then," surmises Kehoe. "And the more people you get together, the bigger the chance of changing the gene pool and going into modern man."

As communal big-game hunters, modern humans in Europe would have required some means of preserving their vast kills from spoilage. While their rock shelters have yet to bare any traces of pemmican making, Kehoe remains optimistic, for a lightweight, backpacking food would help explain the quick spread of modern humans throughout Eurasia. "If Paleolithic humans had the same thing, it would have been a new and different ball game for them," Kehoe concludes.

"They could have moved from Spain and southeastern France all the way into the Russian plains. They would have been able to move quickly and maybe do a lot of trading for their pemmican."

It is a fascinating theory, one that only a plains archaeologist could envisage, but hard data to support or refute it has yet to emerge. Even so, it seems clear that the shadowed prairie of Head-Smashed-In holds vital clues to the long-forgotten past. "We have the Upper Paleolithic ecosystem right outside our door here," says Reeves, leaning back in his chair in his University of Calgary office. "We're dealing with cultures operating over the last 10,000 years in the same environment that operated in Eurasia. So we've got things we can learn here that will give us a much better understanding of cultural evolution during the Upper Paleolithic."

For Reeves and other plains lovers who wander the silent prairies today, searching for bone and reddened buffalo stone, the crumbling coulees and cliffs of southern Alberta are rich in memory. While the thundering hooves of bison, the tempest of their terror, are gone, the sound may echo further back in time than anyone once dreamed.

9

VALE OF TEARS

Ball Site, Ontario

*What shall I say of their strange patience
in their poverty, famine and sickness?*

—FATHER JEAN DE BRÉBEUF

Dean Knight frowns. Tweaking the wilted ends of his mustache into two sharp upright points, he bends over a sturdy metal cabinet, tugging at the drawers. It is a muggy Friday night just outside the tiny village of Warminster, seventy-five miles north of Toronto. In the farmyard beyond, Knight's boisterous crew primps and packs for the weekend. Shaking off the dust of the day at Tent City, they stuff their bags with laundry and hustle off to the city to slake their thirst in shady bars, soak their bones in cool baths. But here, in this double-wide trailer, a makeshift field laboratory, Knight is in no rush to be gone. With a strange tenderness, he lifts out one cardboard box, then another. I peer over his shoulder. Inside nestle more than a dozen arrowheads, each stained dark with verdigris—relics of an ancient collision of two worlds.

Four hundred years ago, this green countryside, with its oak and white pine, elm and maple, flanked the eastern edges of a land known as Huronia. Not far from where Knight and I now stand, a thousand Huron or more passed the bitter winter nights in great longhouses, watching the flames dance back and forth in the darkness. It was a world imbued with spirits and mystical powers. Around the hearths, the old people told tales of Aataentsic, the mother of all, who once fell from her home in the sky to the sea below. Taking pity, the muskrat dove to the water's bottom, scooping up muck and spreading it along the hard shell of a turtle. It became an island home for Aataentsic and her children; in remembrance of this saving grace, those gathered around the longhouse fires here called themselves Wendat—the islanders.

But even as the embers blazed and children slept in their mothers' arms, dreaming of falling from azure skies, the days of island solitude were drawing to a close. Rustling through one of the small cardboard boxes, Knight, a professor of anthropology at Wilfrid Laurier University in Waterloo, Ontario, picks out a handful of brass arrowheads, their hard metal tinkling like so much spare change. I stare down, amazed. Some are thin sheets rolled into sharp cones. Others are cutouts shaped like little Christmas trees. But all are worked scraps of brass from French kettles. I turn them over in my hand. Some 400 years ago, long before the first Europeans stepped foot here, quiet with wonder, the shadow of Old World had already stolen over these forests.

Just what transpired when these remote villagers and others came face-to-face with Europeans is a question that has long haunted scholars. For decades now, a small army of researchers has struggled and strained to glimpse that shadowy moment when prehistory becomes history in North America. It has been a long uphill battle, one fraught with difficulties. The faded parchments of colonists are fragmentary, the archaeology frequently ambiguous. But in the case of the Wendat, or the Huron, as history now knows them, researchers work with a rare advantage: Early French observers in these parts penned dozens of volumes of letters and journals for an avid public. As Bruce Trigger, an authority on early historic cultures in the Eastern Woodlands, once noted, "no other tribe in eastern North America has been described in such minute detail so soon after contact with Europeans" (Trigger 1969).

Indeed, almost from the moment the first official envoy from the Old World, Samuel de Champlain, set foot in Huronia in 1615, pages of rich, florid prose flowed into the historical record. Looking over the narratives of Champlain and others, we learn that the Huron, a confederacy of five tribes, defended a small but fertile band of land dividing Georgian Bay from Lake Simcoe in southern Ontario. Horticulturalists, they pushed the far northern boundaries of prehistoric farming, slashing and burning the hardwood forest to plant corn and other crops. Master traders, they bartered cornmeal and fishnets for the warm furs of neighboring hunting peoples: These they promptly traded to the French for iron axes to clear more fields.

But such prosperity proved fleeting. In 1635, black-robed Jesuit priests dispatched the first of many letters detailing strange and deadly diseases sweeping through Huronia. Five years later, the Jesuits watched in horror as warfare plunged Huronia into despair. Allied closely by trade with northern tribes, the Huron had aroused the enmity of their fellow Iroquoian speakers to the south—the Seneca, Cayuga, Onondaga, Oneida, and Mohawk, collectively known to history as the Five Nations or more often as the Iroquois. In 1640, the hostilities long simmering around the Great Lakes exploded into open warfare: Iroquois warriors razed entire Huron villages, slaughtering all who stood in their way.

It makes for a gripping read, as generations of schoolchildren can attest. But researchers now agree that the seeds of these misfortunes were planted in the early days of contact; the difficulty lies in tracing those obscure encounters. Basque and Breton crews frequented the Gulf of St. Lawrence—a major waterway to the Great Lakes—as early as 1510. And twenty-five years later, Jacques Cartier and his crew strolled through Iroquoian cornfields near present-day Montreal, some 300 miles east of Huronia. In light of such records, scholars now wonder just when Huron tribes first came under the unhealthy influence of Europeans. Could Old World disease have crept from St. Lawrence traders to inland peoples in the 1500s, winnowing Huron numbers long before Champlain and the first colonists arrived? And could such devastation have transformed age-old patterns of warfare?

Eager to glimpse something of this shadowland, Knight began excavations just west of Warminster in the 1970s. And on a sunny July morning, amid a small forest of sensible brown canvas and wild-neon nylon at Tent City, he is still hard at work. A trim, jovial man in his late forties, with straight brown hair, neatly clipped beard, and improbable handlebar mustache, Knight clearly thrives on camp life. Downing the last of a bowl of fruit at the breakfast table, he joins in the general patter over the previous evening's visit to a favorite crew hangout—a karaoke bar in nearby Orillia. "Did anyone else see the tattoos on that one guy?" he asks finally. "The knuckles on one hand said 'love.' On the other, they said 'hat.' Someone had bitten his finger off in a fight."

The table resounds with laughter. Rising to his feet, Knight shakes his head. Grabbing his pack, he begins loading equipment into the backseat of a rust-spattered Volvo. The crew straggles off to find bag lunches and packs. Offering lifts to as many as his car can accommodate, Knight gently coaxes the aging auto to life. Easing it up the hill with all the tenderness its 335,000 miles demands, he pulls up to a wooden picnic bench in a small, shady thicket. In the sloping pasture below, dairy cows graze the low grasses, swishing flies with ropy tails. Swallows swoop and swoon over the grasses. Blue jays chatter from a fringe of trees.

At the turn of the century, antiquarian Andrew Hunter prowled these country roads, scouring fields and questioning local farmers about the Indian pottery and other goods they had turned up while plowing. Not far from where we stand, the residents, noted Hunter in his published report, had scavenged "3 or 4 iron tomahawks, 3 or 4 'skinning stones,' a mealing stone or mortar, some iron arrowheads, pipes, pottery fragments, etc." Intrigued by this and other surveys in the region, Knight stopped here for a look in 1975—just as property owner Don Ball was uprooting several old hawthorn trees. "There were circular holes where they were lifting these trees out," says Knight, leading the way down a well-worn trail, "and I got glass beads and arrowheads and pottery. It was really the thing I was looking for."

Ahead of us, by a small storage trailer, a 10-foot-high stack of shorn branches and severed saplings towers above the northeastern edges of the ancient village. Beyond, dappled by forest shadows, sandpiles rise waist high by two rows of shallow trenches, the current excavations. Stripped of greenery—wild carrot and sweet clover, birch and poplar—the Ball site looks like a giant sandbox. The Huron liked sand. Dependent on their corn crop, they prized land that could be easily tilled with digging sticks. "Glacial Lake Algonquin used to be out there," says Knight, waving a hand toward the north, "so the sandy, loamy soil that we're getting here is the result of the sandy beaches of the lake."

Stringing out across the trenches in pairs, crew members haul out field notes and reach for files to sharpen shovels. While plowshares have churned the ancient house floors of this village into indecipherable chaos, the layers beneath remain largely intact. To trained eyes, large stains betray stor-

Drawing of the Ball site. This illustration was completed before the discovery of additional longhouses: The site is now known to have included at least sixty-nine houses. (Drawing by Ivan Kocsis; courtesy of the Royal Ontario Museum.)

age and refuse pits: Small splotches often mark the spots where house or palisade posts once stood. Spying two students in doubt along the far trench, Knight hurries over for a look. Bending down on hands and knees beside them, he peers down at one partially excavated stain, pointing out the barely perceptible imprint of a house post. "With this light in the morning," he says, smiling, "you can see anything."

It is slow, plodding labor, laced only by good-natured joking and endless speculation. But as the students convey coordinates of posts and pits to the mapping team, the floor plans of two more great longhouses slowly materialize like ghosts on the chart. By such means, says Knight, the team has uncovered a sprawling palisade and sixty-nine longhouses of varying sizes extending over more than nine acres of rolling blufftop. The largest of these wood and bark homes once stretched 130 feet long and 26 feet wide and likely sheltered more than fifty people. "This might represent a chief's house," says Knight.

In such houses, sociable Huron families spent much of the winter, crowding together. Village refuse pits are thick with the detritus of their days—fragments of clay smoking pipes shaped like humans, birds, moose, bear; broken gaming pieces; fragments of ceramic cooking vessels ("they washed them a lot; there's very few that you find burned dinners on," says Knight); deer and fish bones, kernels of corn. And from time to time here, they lost or reluctantly discarded something much more valuable and rare—fifty or so glass beads, an iron axe, scraps of brass kettles rolled into arrowheads, finger rings, and other ornaments.

Like many other researchers, Knight would love to know just when these villagers came by European metal goods. The relative sparsity of axes and other items, he explains, clearly argues for an early date. To narrow down the time range as finely as possible, he has turned to detailed studies of the fifty or so glass beads unearthed in the village middens. Over the past decade or so, colleague William Fitzgerald has scrutinized historical records in Europe, classifying and dating the types of beads early traders commonly carried to New France. After sifting through the collection here, Fitzgerald concluded that the small European baubles had landed in the Ball site as early as the late 1590s—almost two decades before Champlain set foot in Huronia.

And families at the Ball site were not the only ones bartering for European wares in the sixteenth century. Just four miles to the west, Huron families interred their dead with a precious European iron chisel sometime between 1550 and 1580. Further south, along the Trent River in Ontario, villagers amassed scraps of European metal by the mid-1500s. "As soon as the French arrive, it starts to trade in," says Knight. Through their renowned love of trading, the Huron had encountered European culture at least six decades before the dates generally recorded in history books.

Whether a small party of traders from this village shook hands with French sailors along the St. Lawrence River somewhere, eyeing their shaggy beards and woolen doublets as they bartered for a brass kettle, or whether they simply acquired the metal from intermediaries such as the Algonquians is still not clear. But such evidence raises a host of questions. Did European plagues pass as swiftly from hand to hand, sweeping into distant woodland villages before the Europeans themselves? Were the Huron who greeted Champlain so warmly in 1615 the wan shadow of a once far more populous people?

✦ ✦ ✦

Sitting in a small, cluttered, fifth-floor office at the Ministry of Transportation in Toronto, Gary Warrick smiles as he listens to the questions, his glance lighting for a moment on the window. A sandy-haired man of forty-one with intense blue eyes, all-American good looks and a penchant for plain speech, Warrick is one of the rising stars of Iroquoian archaeology, a scholar whose meticulous attention to detail has won the high praise of such authorities as Bruce Trigger. Possessed of a recent doctoral degree in anthropology from McGill University and now employed as an archaeologist by the Ontario government, Warrick has devoted much of the past decade to charting the spread of European contagion among the Huron.

Finds from the Ball site: top left, clay pipes; top right, pipe decorated with a human face; bottom, brass points and iron axe. (Photos by Christopher Gothard, courtesy of Dean Knight.)

Warrick began mulling over the problem in the late 1970s while gathering scraps of brass and copper from an early-seventeenth-century Neutral Confederacy village in Ontario. Wondering whether European viruses had infiltrated inland tribes as swiftly as European trade goods, he began delving into the scientific literature. So convinced were some scholars that they had radically revised pre-Columbian population es-

*Years of excavation at the Ball site have yielded assorted clay pots (top)
and metal tools, such as this iron awl with a bone handle (bottom).
(Photos by Christopher Gothard, courtesy of Dean Knight.)*

timates for the region north of the Rio Grande. Indeed, one highly influential American anthropologist, Henry Dobyns, soon pegged the figure at some 18 million people, sweeping aside estimates based on such sources as seventeenth-century mission censuses. Conservative critics howled: The historical literature put the count closer to 1 million. "So you had these two camps set up and arguing based on very little evidence archaeologically," says Warrick.

Intrigued by the controversy, he began casting around for ways of detecting an early epidemic among the Huron. It was a tricky problem. Diseases such as smallpox and measles leave few scars on human skeletons. And like neutron bombs, they kill without leveling houses or demolishing palisades. But as Warrick thought it over, he could see a possibility. In other parts of the world—Australia, New Zealand, the South Seas Islands—death rates skyrocketed almost immediately after European sailors stepped ashore with a powerful new microbe. Perhaps by measuring Huron numbers accurately over time, he could pin down the date of the first epidemic.

The question was how. Like other researchers, Warrick had noticed something interesting in the journals of Champlain and others—among the Huron, two families shared each longhouse hearth. And it had likely always been so: The Huron word for hearth, *te onatsanhiaj,* meant "something used on two sides." Intrigued, Warrick began counting hearths in all excavated Huron settlements dating from A.D. 900 to 1650. When he was done, he calculated the number per village acre in each century. To his delight, the figure remained relatively constant—as true residential densities are known to do. "Every society has it. We can tolerate a certain degree of crowding but beyond that we experience psychological stress. It's like people from different cultures on the elevator. Some people don't mind crowding, others get upset."

Knowing this average density, he could estimate the number of hearths in reported but unexcavated villages. And by poring over pottery samples gathered from their surfaces, searching for certain stylistic traits, he could date them one by one. After nearly three years of painstaking work, Warrick had amassed precise data for more than 450 Huron villages, each occupied for just twenty years or so before corn crops exhausted the surrounding fields and necessitated a move. It was a major feat. But a critical part of the equation was still missing. To pin down ancient populations, he still needed to know the number of people in average Huron families over time.

The yellowing bones of the dead brimmed with clues. During the early fourteenth century, the Huron had begun celebrating what is now known as the Feast of the Dead. Described graphically by resident Jesuit priests, this great ceremony coincided with the abandonment of a village. In preparation, families exhumed the bodies of their dead from temporary cemetaries bordering the village. Stripping corpses of any last shreds of flesh, they bundled the bones in fine fur robes. On the appointed day, they assembled by a common grave excavated near the old village. There, they emptied the bundles into the ground. "The crowd raised a great cry of lamentation," writes Bruce Trigger in *The Huron: Farmers of the North*. "It was the duty of five or six men, stationed in the pit, to arrange the bones. This was done with poles, and the effect of it was to mingle the bones of different individuals together into a homogeneous mass" (Trigger 1969). In the days that followed, the mourners abandoned the village forever.

Over the past few decades, archaeologists had meticulously exhumed and dated several such ossuaries. And four of them—one each from the fourteenth, fifteenth, sixteenth, and seventeenth centuries—had been carefully analyzed. Physical anthropologists had first sorted through the bones in each, tallying the minimum number of individuals buried there. They had then carefully scrutinized the bones, searching for key diagnostic features that reveal an individual's age at the time of death. For Warrick, such information proved invaluable. By plugging the resulting population profile into the abridged life tables of demographers—similar to the actuarial tables compiled by the life insurance industry—he could calculate the sizes of average Huron families in the fourteenth, fifteenth, sixteenth, and early seventeenth centuries.

One last step remained: to compute Huron populations in each of these centuries. Warrick could scarcely believe the results. Contrary to the theories of many researchers, confederacy populations had leveled off at some 20,000 people in the fifteenth century, remaining steady as a rock until the early seventeenth century. Only in the 1630s—eighty years after European wares first flowed into the region, fifteen years after Champlain and his companions landed here—did Huron numbers suddenly and precipitously collapse. Far from preceding Europeans in Huronia, European viruses had lagged behind. Why?

✦   ✦   ✦

In 1634, as the first winter gales approached and the woods turned blood red in color, the Huron huddled around their fires in quiet desperation. In the great longhouses, men newly returned from the east quickly sickened with some mysterious ailment. Bound to their beds with a high, violent fever, they soon came down with hideous spots. Some went blind, others suffered a wasting form of diarrhea. "It has been so universal among the Savages of our acquaintance," noted Father Jean de Brébeuf in a letter to his superior in Quebec City, "that I do not know if one has escaped its attacks" (Thwaites 1896–1901). In truth, many died from the strange illness. It was measles.

For the Huron, once so healthy and robust that they had excited the envy of Champlain, this terrifying plague was just a taste of horrors to come. In the winter of 1636, influenza crept into the longhouses like a thief, stealing the vigor of the young and elderly. In 1637, scarlet fever, or something much like it, battered Huronia, weakening the young and old. The following year, the most deadly of all epidemics to be visited on the Huron—smallpox—swept through the villages, striking down entire families, one by one. The faces of once beautiful women were reduced to huge open sores; the flesh of the men oozed blood. "The sick smelled horribly of rotting flesh," writes Andrew Nikiforuk in his fascinating account of small-pox (Nikiforuk 1991). In all, one in every two perished.

The accounts, modern and contemporary, make for grue-some, haunting reading. But in poring over them, Warrick couldn't stop wondering why these viruses had failed to sweep through Huronia earlier. Perplexed, he began studying the sci-entific literature on infectious diseases. Contagions such as smallpox and measles, he discovered, confer lifetime immu-nity: After contracting measles once, for example, a person could not come down with the disease again. And both viruses flourished in great cities where they could find a large pool of susceptible victims. In seventeenth-century France, already a highly urbanized nation, smallpox and measles were childhood diseases. And they seldom reaped lives, for the two viruses trig-ger milder symptoms in children than they do in adults.

Had children unwittingly carried these lethal viruses to the New World? Warrick dug into early colonial accounts. In the sixteenth and early seventeenth centuries, European fish-ing boats and trading vessels had carried mainly adult males to New France. Only a few children had accompanied them—certainly not enough to keep an infection alive all the way from Europe. Even in favorable weather, the sailing took a month; to keep a contagion circulating during that period, reasoned Warrick, a ship needed a large pool of susceptible children, one passing the disease to another over the course of the voyage. "I have three kids myself," he says, "and one will bring a flu home and the others might not get it for a week. In-evitably they do, however, they always do."

Warrick returned to the colonial records. He was soon fascinated. In June of 1634, a French sailing vessel packed with young families dropped anchor in the St. Lawrence River. "I think there were thirty kids on that one ship that docked at Quebec City," he says. "And it was that summer that diseases were transmitted to the Montaignais people who lived next door to Quebec City, and transmitted to the trading Huron who brought it all the way back to Huronia. That's when you see the first sign of disease."

In all likelihood, at least one of these children landed carrying the measles virus, which spreads in fine nose or mouth droplets. "All that it would have taken is for one of those Hurons to get close to that kid," observes Warrick. "And they would have been interested in kids. It's the first time they saw them. It would have been—'oh, look these people have children.' I think there would have been a sort of fascination with these little blond-haired French kids—and they would have been blond at age three or four. The parents wouldn't have thought anything of letting these native people close to these sick kids."

In Huronia, the viruses spread with deadly ease. Among the great longhouses, sixty or so people rubbed elbows under one roof: The contagion danced from one to another effortlessly. "It was the worst possible scenario for the introduction of a European disease," says Warrick. And even the compassion of a niece for a dying uncle, a grandparent for a feverish child, stole lives. Unlike Europeans who tended to shun the ill, quarantining them during epidemics such as the Black Death, the Huron rallied around the sick and dying, attempting to minister to their needs. "They didn't realize that they were in fact catching the disease themselves," says Warrick, "and then taking it back to their own longhouses."

The epidemics repeatedly struck at the worst of all possible times, moreover. Returning during late summer from their forays to posts at Montreal or Quebec City, trading parties often infected their home villages during the critical fall harvest. Too weak to walk out to their fields, people were unable to store corn for the winter; famine soon stalked in the footsteps of plague. Opportunistic infections such as pneumonia then ruthlessly felled the young and the elderly. "You see, you generally don't die from the initial disease," says Warrick. "A lot of people have the idea that the native people had such raging fevers that they died: That's not true. It was just that everyone got sick at the same time." In all, two of every three Huron succumbed to the potent blend of imported viruses and miscellaneous infections—a mortality rate double that suffered during the dreaded Black Death in Europe. By 1640, only 7,800 Huron remained.

The survivors could scarcely believe their eyes. In some longhouses where a hundred people had once laughed and argued, their voices rising in a buzzing murmur, only two or three children sat silently, too stunned and frightened to cry. No one could quite believe what happened. While some suggested that the plagues had boiled forth from the shiny French kettles, others theorized that Champlain, who had died in 1635, intended to take the Huron with him. For all, however, the grief proved almost intolerable. "It's really heart-wrenching," says Warrick. "You can just imagine these people with vacant stares walking around the villages."

✦   ✦   ✦

In the stillness of a Sunday afternoon, I duck into the cool darkness of a longhouse at Ste. Marie Among the Hurons. Along the center of the floor, shafts of silver slant down from the smokeholes like great spotlights. Along the high rafters, cobs of corn hang in neat rows; furs and pelts lie scattered over the tops of boxes along the sleeping benches. The rich smokiness of campfires lingers in the air. Alone here, beneath a ceiling that stretches 20 feet high, I have the sudden feeling that I am standing in a cathedral.

Built in 1639 some twenty miles northwest of the Ball site, Ste. Marie was a Jesuit mission. Reconstructed by the Ontario government in the 1960s, after archaeologists Kenneth Kidd and William Jury uncovered part of the mission foundations, Ste. Marie witnessed some of the darkest hours of what historians now call the Iroquois War. It was here, in 1649, that many panic-stricken Huron fled after Iroquois forces razed two of their largest villages, slaughtered many, and sentenced two French priests, Jean de Brébeuf and Gabriel Lalemant, to death by ritual torture. Today, Brébeuf, Lalemant, and three other Jesuit priests are honored up the hill in a massive gray stone chapel, the Martyrs' Shrine.

Such devastating warfare, which began around 1640, marked a new phase in the rancorous relations between the Huron and their Five Nations enemies. For nearly two centuries, the two confederacies had avenged personal grievances and battled over territorial rights to the all-important deer-hunting grounds. (Without a generous supply of deer hides for winter clothing, a family in the region could scarcely venture outdoors in winter without risk of freezing.) But despite the large size of the war parties, these early hostilities amounted mainly to raiding—as Champlain discovered to his astonishment in 1615.

Recruited to the Huron cause, the French merchant and his men accompanied a party south to New York State. Arriving at last in enemy territory, the Huron captured a small Iroquois fishing party and exchanged blows with Iroquois warriors outside the village. To the seventeenth-century Europeans, fully versed in all the niceties of slaughter and seige warfare, such skirmishes seemed a paltry waste of time. "This prompted me to speak out to them," writes Champlain, "and to use some very hard and unpleasant words, in order to incite them to do their duty" (Bigger 1922). Ever mindful of the need to please the wealthy Frenchman, the Huron at last descended on the village with seige equipment of Champlain's design. But just as the Huron forces were about to breach the palisade walls, they jettisoned the imported equipment. All at once, noted Champlain, they "began to shout at the enemy, shooting arrows into the fort, which in my opinion did no great harm to the enemy."

In 1640, however, skirmishes in village cornfields came to an abrupt end. Iroquois warriors embraced a style of warfare that Europeans could understand much better: They assaulted villages, smashed through timber palisades, and spread terror wherever they tread. Scholars have long wondered why. Many lay the blame with the European fur trade. After decades of determined trapping in their own territory, the Iroquois had almost extinguished beaver and other furbearing animals in Upper New York State. By the late 1630s, they were desperate for a new supply. Iroquois leaders soon cast their covetous eyes north to the profitable fur trade that the Huron had established with the Algonquians and other hunting peoples. By destroying the Huron, leaving not a village standing, the Iroquois could control vastly extended hunting territories, ensuring a steady torrent of trade goods—especially the muskets they needed to protect themselves.

This trade theory explains much. But Warrick now believes something else drove the Iroquois, too. The new phase of warfare, he notes, closely follows the first great wave of European epidemics through the Great Lakes area. It is quite possible that the fabled Iroquois war parties battled more for captives than they did for furs. Surrounded by hostile tribes, decimated by Old World viruses, the Iroquois simply could not survive in the 1640s without an immediate transfusion of men, women, and children. "The Iroquois were so depopulated," says Warrick, "they had to look farther afield to replenish their numbers basically. It wasn't just for furs. Over and over again you see that in the raids on the Huron—they didn't take away furs, they took people."

On some occasions, the Iroquois rounded up whole villages. In 1649, for example, the Petun tribe—a close ally of the Huron—received word that an Iroquois raiding party had stolen into their territory. "So all the men from the main village of Etharita went out to intercept them, thinking 'we're far superior in numbers and if we find these guys we'll teach them a lesson,'" says Warrick. "And they missed them. The Iroquois circled around them and they found all the women and children in the village. So they took the entire village captive and paraded them back to a Five Nations village. The Petun men got back three days later, and the accounts were that they just sat on logs, staring off into space."

Once at home, the Iroquois guarded the captives closely to ensure no one escaped. And some Huron soon settled in to the life of a Seneca or Mohawk village, adopted as family members. "Really there wouldn't have been much difference to the Huron living in the Five Nations at that time. It's their own culture. And I'm sure that some Hurons knew that the Huron Confederacy didn't have long to go, that they were a shattered nation. And you'd either go with the French and become French, or continue to be an Iroquoian. Be proud of your Iroquoian heritage, regardless of being Huron, Seneca, or Mohawk." Indeed in some cases, captives rose to positions of power in their adopted tribes; one ultimately became a leader of the Onondaga Nation.

At home in Huronia, the remaining villages tried to preserve calm and order. But after years of hemorrhaging human lives, they could barely stand. With the end in sight, Huron chiefs gathered together in their councils, deliberating on the future. While some proposed leading their followers to the Ohio valley, others planned to accompany the Jesuits on their retreat east to Quebec. By 1650, shadowy elm, maple, and oak forests began taking root again in the abandoned cornfields of Huronia; the villages were given over to ghosts.

✦   ✦   ✦

But the Huron, children of the hapless woman who fell from the sky, never forgot their cornfields and longhouses. Looking back on the past, they still shake their heads at the speed with which they were dispossessed of nearly all they once loved. In his office at the Saskatchewan Indian Federation College in Regina, Georges Sioui, whose Wendat name *Wendayete* means "the one who carries an island on his back," can still scarcely believe the swift catastrophe that followed on the heels of Europeans in Huronia. "We lost our country very fast," he says in a soft voice. "In 1615, the Europeans began arriving in numbers and thirty-five years later, in 1650, it was all over with. Our country was destroyed and our homes and tribes were dispersed. The strength of the land and the principle of organization of all those tribes and nations were destroyed in just thirty-five years."

Today, says Sioui, an eloquent and ardent native activist with a doctoral degree in history from Laval University, just 5,000 or so Huron survive—most in Oklahoma and Quebec, and smaller, scattered numbers in Ohio, California, Mexico, and New York State. But conscious as they are of all they have lost, they are far from humbled. In recent years, Sioui and his family battled for rights to a centuries-old hunting ground in Quebec, taking their case all the way to the Supreme Court of Canada: They won. And Sioui still takes fierce pride in all those who uphold the traditions of the past. Oral history, he says, is clear. "It is still said that most of our people died from disease brought over from Europe. We were overpowered not by the enemy, the enemy was never able to do us any harm. Diseases brought us down."

Conclusion

In the soft afternoon light, I stare up at a thicket of cedar poles carved in the likenesses of spirits. Chiseled a hundred years ago and more by Haida, Kwakiutl, and Tsimshian artists along the west coast of Canada and bathed in golden light, the cracked and splintered totem poles tower 30 feet and more above my head. They look like the sculptured guardians of some ancient Egyptian temple. In the stillness of this lofty museum gallery in Vancouver, where voices are reduced to hushed murmurings, the faces of these spirits peer out alert, powerful, watchful—and above all haunting. Flanking the aisles like messengers from the past, these poles are potent reminders of the mystery and wonder of the ancient cultures that first greeted Europeans on this continent.

Standing here, gazing up at carvings of bears and sea wolves, thunderbirds and sea lions, I marvel once again at the cultural myopia of early Europeans along this coast. A hundred and fifty years or so ago, as missionaries and traders trickled into the remote native villages of the Queen Charlotte Islands and the Nass River valley, a kind of blindness descended upon them. In their letters and journals, they described the inhabitants of Kitwancool and Skidegate as savages and heathens, lacking all that was necessary for civilized life—complex religion, written language, and a wage economy. Almost at once, Anglican missionaries such as Robert Tomlinson began hatching plans to "change the natives from ignorant, bloodthirsty cruel savages into quiet useful subjects of our gracious Queen" (Fisher 1977). Seeing little value in traditional culture, they set to work recasting the villagers in their own image—prim Victorians who obeyed Christian scripture, worked for wages, and entrusted their children to strangers in government schools.

Today, we have all come to realize just how destructive these missionizing and westernizing efforts were. Historians and anthropologists have chronicled the social tragedies that so often followed upon the near-obliteration of ancient native languages and religions and millennia-old patterns of hunting and fishing; outspoken native activists across North America have raised public awareness of the importance and value of traditional cultures. And they continue to do so. But we still have a long way to go in understanding—and truly seeing—the continent's most ancient cultures. Although we now possess powerful corrective lenses in the form of history and archaeology, we have developed, I believe, new blind spots.

It has become increasingly fashionable in recent years, for example, to portray the ancient Americas as a kind of paradise on earth. Deeply troubled by the violence, materialism, and disorder of modern North American society, many popular writers have begun casting longing glances at the distant past. In the prehistoric Americas, argue such influential writers as Kirkpatrick Sale, a founder of the New York Green Party, tribal groups lived in harmony with nature and with each other. Evils such as warfare, slavery, overpopulation, and environmental destruction were unknown. "Tribal life does not have these mythical downsides . . ." notes Sale confidently in a recent interview in *Wired*. "Tribes have long-established practices to keep themselves harmonious and stable, including the practice of birth control so as not to exceed the carrying capacity of the places where they live" (Sale and Kelly 1995). Only the arrival of Europeans in the late fifteenth century, he suggests, destroyed this perfect balancing act.

Such simplistic portraits of the past, I believe, strip ancient tribal cultures of their basic humanity. They transform what were once real men, women, and children into saints and turn the prehistory of the continent into a kind of hagiography. But archaeology offers little support for such a utopia: Indeed it refutes such notions. At Eel Point in southern California, for example, sea hunters clearly began plundering the environment as early as 1,000 years ago. Faced with burgeoning populations, they fished as if there were no tomorrow, wiping out key species and reducing one of the world's most productive ecosystems to a bleak barren. And acts of ruthless violence were far from unknown in the ancient Americas, as discoveries at Cahokia or at Anasazi settlements surrounding Chaco Canyon now demonstrate. In other words, life was complex then, too. Basic human nature prevailed.

Other writers and scholars have fallen prey to what I think of as the numbers game—population estimates. During the 1950s, social scientists came to see population density as a major index of cultural development: The more numerous and crowded together humans were, the more highly developed their culture would likely be. Influenced by this thinking, scholars such as American ethnohistorian Henry Dobyns began reexamining—and greatly boosting—prehistoric population figures in the New World. While earlier researchers pegged the population of Canada and the United States at approximately 1 million in 1492, Dobyns soon pushed the figure to 18 million, all the time edging out on very thin scholarly ice. Intrigued, a host of popular writers latched on to Dobyns' estimates, little interested in how he arrived at them.

As it turns out, Dobyns' basic premise—that European diseases preceded European emissaries throughout the New World—is riddled with holes. And recent research is giving many experts pause for thought. While many liberal scientists contend that as many as 10 million people lived north of Mexico in the late fifteenth century, archaeologists such as Warrick suggest the figure is much closer to 2 to 3 million. Their work makes a great deal of sense to me. And decades of careful research now shows us that population is no sure guide to cultural development. Indeed, even in areas of relatively low population density, rich and sophisticated cultures arose. Take the case of the high Arctic. Boasting one of the lowest population densities in the continent—if not the lowest—it nevertheless fostered several highly accomplished cultures, including the prehistoric Dorset. A deeply religious people, the Dorset were master artists, carving ivory miniatures of bears, seals, and loons that are marvels of human design. But the Dorset possessed many other skills that give us pause for thought today. Armed with a finely honed knowledge of animal behavior, they regularly stalked caribou, musk ox, walrus, and polar bear, and skillfully organized hunts of one of the most dangerous of all marine prey: whales. These are not the hallmarks of primitive life.

Indeed, what North American archaeology now demonstrates with increasing clarity is that nothing is as simple as researchers once thought it was. The strange and diverse cultures of this continent are far older, far more ingenious, and far more successful than earlier scholarship ever hinted. In every major sphere of prehistoric life, from economics to politics and religion, researchers from the icy coasts of Alaska to the everglades of Florida are uncovering a new and unexpected sophistication.

This is particularly true of the current debate over the peopling of the continent. Until very recently, archaeologists widely agreed that Siberian migrants first trekked across the frozen reaches of Beringia to the New World some 12,000 years ago. It was only then, at the tail end of the last glaciation, reasoned experts, that modern humans had mastered the necessary skills for Arctic survival. But increasingly, North American researchers are arguing for earlier and earlier dates, based on new findings. In the northern Yukon, for example, Jacques Cinq-Mars has uncovered intriguing evidence of human hunters at Bluefish Caves some 23,000 years ago—at the very peak of the last glaciation. And as he points out, new radiocarbon dates from mammoth-bone tools unearthed along the Old Crow River strongly suggest a human presence there some 40,000 years ago.

The implications of these early dates are stunning. If small bands of hunters truly arrived in the northern Yukon sometime between 23,000 and 40,000 years ago, they had clearly adapted to bitter Arctic winters far earlier than previous researchers credited. And these migrants may well have represented the vanguard of a major human revolution sweeping the Old World. It is at just this moment in time, some 40,000 years ago, that bands of modern humans, *Homo sapiens*, were springing up throughout Europe and parts of Asia, while the indigenous Neanderthals were vanishing. Long regarded as isolated from these major Paleolithic developments, North America may be intimately linked to them.

Less controversial but equally fascinating are the new lines of inquiry relating to ancient economies. For years, researchers greatly underrated the ability of many prehistoric hunting cultures to wrest a living from the land. On the northern plains, for example, scholars long believed that bison hunters managed only a meager existence before the arrival of European horses in the 1700s. (Ice Age horses had died out in North America some 10,000 years earlier.) Without mounts, went the reasoning, bison hunters would have encountered grave difficulties in maneuvering large and skittish herds of bison over narrow stretches of cliffs.

Current scientific research, however, serves up a very different image. As early as the third millennium B.C., pedestrian hunters were luring great bison herds over the cliffs at Head-Smashed-In, making skillful use of everything from natural topography, optical illusion, and the blinding rays of dawn. And over time, hunters there built an intricate network of more than thirty intersecting drive lanes, many to take advantage of subtle shifts in the wind. Today, experts call Head-Smashed-In one of the most brilliant prehistoric hunting traps in the world. And bands clearly made the most of it. By the first century A.D., they began laboriously rendering buffalo bone grease for a major export—pemmican.

And prehistoric hunter-gatherers were equally adroit in wresting a living from the water. During the early decades of this century, most scholars believed that early coastal dwellers were simple beachcombers, idlers who passed their days on shore digging clams and other shellfish. But in recent years, armed with the new science of faunal analysis, researchers have begun unearthing a fascinating tale of hunting and fishing acumen along the California coast. At Eel Point, for example, marine bands began fishing intensively as early as 4,700 years ago, ingeniously working every conceivable inshore ocean ecosystem—from the kelp beds and sandy clearings to the deep submarine canyons. And it now seems likely that they began hunting some of the world's swiftest and most intelligent sea mammals—dolphins—more than 1,000 years ago.

Research on the continent's ancient farming cultures abounds in surprises as well. For years, most archaeologists believed that the origins of all early North American agriculture could be traced back to Mexico. Indeed, most researchers agreed that the first crop north of the Rio Grande was a tropical cultigen—maize. And such theories fit well with popular cultural prejudices. As the founders of populous, impressive city-states, Mesoamerican peoples were deemed to be the natural propagators of ideas: Cultures north of the Rio Grande, far sparser in population, were widely regarded as passive recipients.

Nothing, however, could be further from the truth, as the elegant research of Bruce Smith now demonstrates. By examining seeds recovered from prehistoric sites with a scanning electron microscope, Smith found that bands in the eastern woodlands had domesticated wild plants such as squash, sunflower, and goosefoot as early as 3,000 to 4,000 years ago—a good millennium before traders arrived bearing maize. By Hopewell times, some bands in the eastern United States relied extensively on the high yields of their homegrown produce. And even when sweet-tasting corn finally swept the region, becoming the crop of choice in the ninth century, many prehistoric farmers continued to plant small plots of native plants. Far from being a passive recipient of ideas, the eastern woodlands now constitutes one of the world's independent centers of plant cultivation.

And what is equally intriguing is the intimate relationship that soon developed between farmer and hunter in prehistoric North America. Traditionally, archaeologists on the continent considered hunting and farming peoples as two very separate entities, each self-sufficient and distinct. But in-

creasingly, researchers are beginning to see a more complicated picture. At Head-Smashed-In, for example, hunters became dealers in bison products as early as 2,000 years ago,
and one likely market for their goods lay in the agricultural
communities to the east. Indeed, the discovery of Mississippian shell artifacts in the Sweetgrass Hills of northern Montana now suggests at least an indirect link between these
bison hunters and the Mississippian people—possibly the inhabitants of Cahokia.

An even closer trading relationship flourished between
the farming Huron and the hunting Algonquian peoples during the sixteenth century. As maize farmers at the northern
limits of prehistoric agriculture in North America, the Huron
regularly traded their surplus corn for the furs of northern
hunters. (As a storable food, corn could ward off starvation
in late winter, when all other food reserves were exhausted.)
But as current research now shows, the far-flung trading
missions of the Huron resulted in tragedy in the early seventeenth century. As prosperous go-betweens in the European
fur trade, the Huron undertook annual expeditions to
French settlements in Quebec. And it was there, suggests
Gary Warrick, in the summer of 1634, that a French child
first infected Huron traders with what was likely measles—
the first of several devastating European epidemics to deci-
mate the tribe.

While Warrick and others continue to unravel the strange
twists and turns of prehistoric economic life on the continent,
others turn their attention to ancient social and political in-
stitutions—with telling results. For years, researchers have
wondered what conditions first gave rise to inequality in
hunter-gatherer peoples. Ethnographic research, for example,
shows that most generalized hunter-gatherers are egalitari-
ans. While they may give more weight to the opinions of some
band members than others, they are subject to the rule of
none. Moreover, they share food and possessions freely. Why,
then, did social inequality arise? Why did some people ascend
a social ladder to wealth and power in prehistoric North
America, while others sunk into poverty?

Along the interior plateau of British Columbia, Brian Hayden has uncovered one route to power in a bountiful land. At Keatley Creek, he found that the inhabitants of large and prosperous houses dined on several salmon species some 1,100 years ago, including the most desirable of all—chinook. Residents of the smallest houses made do with just the least desirable species—the pink salmon. Further research shows that the wealthy owned several prized resources, including the best places to fish along the river. They then handed these hereditary rights down to their children. The poor, by contrast, owned next to nothing: They had to make do with the catch from public fishing areas. In all likelihood, suggests Hayden, the seeds of inequality were planted around 3,000 years ago, when hunter-gatherers began specializing in salmon fishing. Guaranteed of catching all the food they needed in a good year, most people raised no objections when an ambitious person staked out a private fishing reserve. But private property, suggests Hayden, soon brought wealth and power. These in turn fostered class consciousness.

Elsewhere on the continent, archaeologists are unearthing the origins of more elaborate forms of social and political organization. At Cahokia, the largest capital ever to rise north of the Rio Grande, Tim Pauketat has revealed the intricate workings of prehistory. Through a meticulous analysis of residential debris in one ancient Cahokia neighborhood, Pauketat has discerned the ascent of a great and powerful lord. At the very beginning of the eleventh century, he now suggests, someone seized power in this Mississippian center, capturing and executing rivals before burying them in Mound 72. Unencumbered then by opposition, he began founding a powerful capital, convincing residents to embark on massive public works such as ceremonial plazas and temple mounds. As time passed, this charismatic lord and his unknown successors assumed the mantle of divinity, becoming local gods and ruling a powerful theocracy until Cahokia finally fell at the end of the thirteenth century.

But the people of Cahokia were not alone in their devout beliefs. One of the recurring themes in North American archaeology relates to the profound importance of religion in ancient life. For years, however, scholars devoted little serious study to the subject; prehistoric cultures north of the Rio Grande, after all, had left no written records of their beliefs and doctrines. It seemed an intractable mystery. But increasingly, archaeologists are turning up other records of religious thought. Cave art is a prime case in point. With clues from the ethnographic literature, researchers such as Solveig Turpin, Carolyn Boyd, and Anna Sofaer are deciphering long-mysterious cave paintings and rock engravings. And like the ancient codices of Mexico, these records are beginning to reveal ancient and rich systems of belief.

Within the Lower Pecos region, for example, Turpin has found 4,200-year-old cave paintings of shamans, a mystical elite who journeyed to the otherworld in trances to intercede with spirits. By studying these fading images with meticulous care, she has discovered representations of many aspects of shamanistic faith, including belief in shape-shifting, the birdlike flight of the soul, and caves as sacred portals. Intriguingly, one recurrent image in the Lower Pecos region portrays shamans transforming into mountain lions—the most powerful feline predator in the area. And this image clearly echoes ancient representations of shamanism in the Old World: At the European rock shelter of Hohlenstein-Stadel, for example, archaeologists recovered a 30,000-year-old carving of a human being transforming into a lion. So current evidence suggests strongly that Eurasian migrants carried shamanism with them when they first arrived on this continent.

Ancient religion, moreover, clearly inspired some of the continent's most impressive prehistoric architecture and public works. As Sofaer's work demonstrates, the Anasazi once viewed Chaco Canyon as the sacred Middle Place—the very spot where the cardinal directions converged and where the earliest pueblo people settled after a long migration. So fundamental was this concept to ancient canyon life, says Sofaer, that Anasazi architects encoded this spatial symbolism in the greathouse of Pueblo Bonito, constructing the center wall along a true north-south line and the principal outer wall along a true east-west line. Where these walls intersected lay the Middle Place. Other monumental works in the canyon represented additional features of the sacred landscape. In all likelihood, the Great North Road recalled the route of ancient migration from the *shipapu,* a sacred hole in the earth from which the Anasazi first clambered up into the light of day.

And as Sofaer and hundreds of other field-workers build increasingly on these findings, interpreting and deciphering new scraps of evidence, the picture of prehistoric life in North America grows ever more tantalizing. Each year, researchers devise dozens of new ways of wresting long-lost information from obscurity, of turning bones and stones into flesh and blood, idea and belief. Each year, the emerging portrait of prehistory grows more complicated, more subtly colored, more finely shaded. And as I watch this image gradually materialize, like some great photograph in silver nitrate, I marvel at the increasingly fine degree of resolution.

Even so, the amount of work that lies ahead is truly staggering. In some parts of the continent, such as the subarctic (a vast swath of land that arcs across Canada from the Pacific Coast to the Atlantic), field-workers have scarcely begun surveying for sites, much less investigating and excavating them. And as the battle for scarce scientific funding grows ever more difficult, the prospects for work in such remote regions grow smaller. Archaeological excavation and analysis, after all, is a very expensive proposition. It becomes even more costly when research teams must rely on helicopters and bush planes for their transport. And public purse strings grow tighter every day.

But without such research, we will never learn the histories of those who preceded us on this continent. Archaeologists will never redeem the promise of their science. The value of archaeology, after all, can far exceed pure scientific knowledge, as excavations at sites such as Ozette in Washington State have demonstrated. Located along the outer coast of the Olympic Peninsula, Ozette was once a village of whalers and sea hunters. In the late 1960s, researchers from Washington State University arrived there to begin excavation. They were soon amazed. Deeply buried beneath a layer of fine clay were the remains of a 450-year-old village destroyed by a catastrophic mudslide—just as the oral history of the Makah said it was.

Saturated with water, the ancient village of Ozette was a true time capsule of the Makah people at the very height of their power as whalers and sea hunters. Enlisting the help of Makah students, researchers began carefully troweling through the ruins. Within the buried houses lay all the worldly goods of early-sixteenth-century Makah families— wooden halibut hooks, harpoons, whistles, gambling pieces, combs, baskets, mats, wooden clubs, canoe paddles, bentwood boxes. Members of the Makah tribe were fascinated. Indeed, elders soon began identifying objects that they had only heard about as children.

To preserve these cherished relics, the Makah and their supporters built a museum nearby at Neah Bay. Today, this museum and the rich cultural history that it contains have become a source of renewal for the Makah people. To write about this cultural resurgence recently for *Federal Archeology*, Roger Friedman interviewed several tribal members. "We are one of the only tribes left on the peninsula that has kept its culture," Yvette McGimpsey told him. "A lot of tribes have lost theirs and are now struggling to get it back. The museum has helped everyone remember who they are. With that here, it's impossible to forget" (Friedman 1995).

For all of us, I suggest, archaeology retrieves a buried and lost past. It reminds us powerfully of what was. Over the past 20,000 years and more on this continent, hundreds of cultures have waxed and waned, each possessing its own vision of the land, its own style of art and ornament, its own way of nurturing the young and burying the dead. Over the past 20,000 years and more, prophets and charlatans, sages and fools, scoundrels and sirens inhabited this land. Archaeology alone has the power to bring them back to life, to restore them to memory and to fill the pages of a new kind of history: prehistory.

As I think of this, I am reminded finally of something an archaeologist once told me about the Hohokam people. A desert-loving folk who diverted river water to raise corn in

southern Arizona, the Hohokam honored their dead by cre-
mating them. Among their ritual paraphernalia, researchers
often find small stone rectangles that resemble picture
frames. For years, baffled researchers theorized that these objects were paint palettes, for crystals of glittering lead ore
often coat the inner area. But a few years ago, an artist in Arizona arrived at another idea. When lead ore is heated, he explained, it turns from gray to bright red. In the flames of a
funeral pyre, the outer frame would become blackened, but
the inner rectangle would turn brilliant fire-red—an open
doorway to another realm.

To me, that is an apt metaphor for archaeology. It is a doorway to another realm, to a past that beckons, ever mysterious.

Further Readings

R eaders interested in a thorough overview of North American archaeology should try *Ancient North America: The Archaeology of a Continent* (1991). Written by well-known California archaeologist Brian Fagan and published by Thames and Hudson, Inc., in New York, *Ancient North America* ranges over the length and breadth of the continent's prehistory.

Those readers keen on trekking to some of the public sites mentioned in this book would do well to pick up a copy of the fourth revised edition of *America's Ancient Treasures: A Guide to Archaeological Sites and Museums in the United States and Canada* (1993) by Franklin Folsom and Mary Elting Folsom. Published by University of New Mexico Press in Albuquerque, *America's Ancient Treasures* is replete with clear directions and helpful background information for sites scattered as far north as Alaska and as far south as Florida. Armchair travelers, on the other hand, might prefer the *Atlas of Ancient America* (reprinted 1989) written by Michael Coe, Dean Snow, and Elizabeth Benson and published in New York by Facts on File.

Introduction

Two fine books—one recent and the other a classic—explore the peculiar history of North American archaeology. *Mound Builders of Ancient America* (1968) written by Robert Silverberg and published by New York Graphic Society Ltd. in Greenwich skillfully examines the controversy that simmered for much of the nineteenth century over the identity of the mound builders. *A History of Archaeological Thought* (1989), written by Bruce Trigger and published in Cambridge by Cambridge University Press, deftly traces the development of key archaeological ideas in North America and elsewhere.

Dark Passages

Readers eager to delve more deeply into early humans and their migrations should take a look at an excellent recent book—*The First Humans: Human Origins and History to 10,000 B.C.* (1993) edited by Goran Burenhult and published in San Francisco by HarperSan Francisco. Those wishing to learn more about the work of Jacques Cinq-Mars will enjoy *Ancient Canada* (1989). Written by archaeologist Robert McGhee and published by the Canadian Museum of Civilization in Hull, *Ancient Canada* explores several of the early cultures that thrived north of the 49th parallel.

Ultramarine

For a colorful look at the hidden ecology of a kelp forest, try Howard Hall's slender book, *The Kelp Forest* (1990), published in San Luis Obispo by Blake Publishing. And for an engaging account of prehistoric life on the Channel Islands, readers should begin with *A Step into the Past: Island Dwellers of Southern California* (1989), published by California State University at Fullerton and edited by J. Smull and T. Cox.

The Rapture

To my mind, the most beautiful book on the Lower Pecos art is *The Rock Art of Texas Indians* (1967), published by the University of Texas Press in Austin. Featuring the exquisite watercolor paintings of Forrest Kirkland and a thoughtful text by William Newcombe, this book is truly haunting. But readers will also enjoy another superlative offering—*Pecos River Rock Art: A Photographic Essay* (1991), published in San Antonio by Sandy McPherson Publishing Company. Written by

Solveig Turpin and illustrated with the inimitable photography of Jimmy Zintgraff, *Pecos River Rock Art* is a delight from start to finish.

The Nouveaux Riches

For a taste of what life was once like at Keatley Creek, readers could hardly do better than to browse the ethnographic writings of James Teit. The most relevant of these works, "The Lillooet Indians," *Memoirs, American Museum of Natural History* (vol. 2) was published in 1906 and edited by none other than the renowned anthropologist Franz Boas.

True Believers

Some of the best recent general-interest writing on the Hopewell has appeared in magazines. Archaeologist David Brose, a Hopewell scholar, has recently published a wonderful piece, "East of the Sun and West of the Moon" in *Rotunda*, vol. 27, 1994 (pp. 10–17). And in 1991, Bruce Smith penned a "Harvest of Prehistory" in *The Sciences*, May/June issue (pp. 30–35).

Desert Prophets

Those intrigued by Anasazi astronomy may want to take a look at *Living the Sky: The Cosmos of the American Indian* (1984). Written by R. A. Williamson and published in Boston by Houghton Mifflin, *Living the Sky* remains a classic study of prehistoric astronomy on this continent. Those wishing to learn more about Anasazi roads should track down a copy of the January/February 1994 issue of *Archaeology*. In "Spirit Paths of the Anasazi" (pp. 36–42), writer John Wicklein succinctly describes current research on these mysterious avenues.

Lord of the Black Drink

Nearly half a century ago, John Witthoft wrote a remarkably comprehensive account of the Green Corn Ceremony. Published as "Green Corn Ceremonialism in the Eastern Wood-lands," *Occasional Contributions from the Museum of Anthropology of the University of Michigan,* no. 13 (1949), Witthoft's work gathers together several early European travelers' accounts of this important festival. And readers interested in plunging into the scholarly literature on Cahokia could scarcely do better than pick up a copy of Tim Pauketat's new book, *The Ascent of Chiefs: Cahokia and Mississippian Politics in Native North America* (1994), published in Tuscaloosa by the University of Alabama Press.

Killing Fields

A solid introduction to the prehistoric bison-hunting cultures of the northern plains is a work by Canadian journalist Liz Bryan. Published in 1991 by The University of Alberta Press in Edmonton, *The Buffalo People: Prehistoric Archaeology on the Canadian Plains,* neatly straddles the gap between academic and popular writing.

Vale of Tears

Native Canadian historian Georges Sioui offers a different perspective on Huronia, examining European contact from the Huron point of view in *For an Amerindian Autohistory* (1992). Published in Montreal by McGill-Queens University Press, Sioui's book draws on Huron oral history and tradition to challenge European accounts. Readers interested in tracing the effects of European contact elsewhere on the globe will find a fascinating chapter, "The Clash of Cultures," in *New World and Pacific Civilizations: Cultures of America, Asia and the Pacific,* edited by Goran Burenhult and published in 1994 by Harper-San Francisco.

Bibliography

Anderson, E. F. 1980. *Peyote: The Divine Cactus.* Tucson and London: The University of Arizona Press.

Benditt, J. 1988. Earlier Americans. *Scientific American.* June, 1988, pp. 28–29.

Benedict, R. 1935. *Zuni Mythology,* Columbia University Contributions to Anthropology, vol. 21. Reprint (2 vols.). New York: AMS Press, 1969.

Biggar, H. P., ed. 1922–1936. *The Works of Samuel de Champlain.* 6 vols. The Champlain Society, Toronto.

Black, F. L. 1992. "Why Did They Die?" *Science* 258: 1739–40.

Bonnichsen, R. 1979. *Pleistocene Bone Technology in the Beringian Refugium.* National Museum of Man Mercury Series, no. 89. Ottawa: National Museums of Canada.

Bordes, F. 1968. *The Old Stone Age.* Translated by J. E. Anderson. New York: McGraw-Hill.

Bower, B. 1990. "America's Talk: The Great Divide." *Science News,* June 9, 1990. pp. 360–362.

Boyd, C. "Shamanic Journeys into the Otherworld of the Archaic Chichimec," *Latin American Antiquity,* in press.

———. 1993. "Pictographic Evidence of the Peyote Cult in the Lower Pecos Archaic." Paper presented at the Shamanism and Rock Art Symposium, February 1993, at San Antonio, Texas.

Boyd, C., and Dering, J. P. 1994. "Medicinal and Hallucinogenic Plants Identified in the Sediments and Pictographs of the Lower Pecos, Texas Archaic." Paper presented at the *59th Annual Meeting of the Society for American Archaeology,* 20–24 April 1994, at Anaheim, California.

Brink, J. 1990. "Bison Butchering and Food Processing at Head-Smashed-In Buffalo Jump, Alberta." Paper presented at the *48th Annual Plains Anthropological Conference*, November 1990, in Oklahoma City, Oklahoma.

Brink, J., and Dawe, B. 1986. *Final Report of the 1984 Field Season at Head-Smashed-In Buffalo Jump, Alberta.* Archaeological Survey of Alberta Manuscript Series No. 9. Edmonton: Alberta Culture.

———. 1989. *Final Report of the 1985 and 1986 Field Season at Head-Smashed-In Buffalo Jump, Alberta.* Archaeological Survey of Alberta Manuscript Series No. 16. Edmonton: Alberta Culture and Multiculturalism.

Brink. J., Wright, M., Dawe, B., and Glaum, D. 1985. *Final Report of the 1983 Field Season at Head-Smashed-In Buffalo Jump, Alberta.* Archaeological Survey of Alberta Manuscript Series No. 1. Edmonton: Alberta Culture.

Brodzky, A. T., Danesewich, R., and Johnson, N. 1977. *Stones, Bones and Skin: Ritual and Shamanic Art.* Toronto: Society for Art Publications.

Brose, D. S. 1994. "East of the Sun and West of the Moon." *Rotunda* vol. 27: 10–17.

Brose, D. S., and Greber, N. 1979. *Hopewell Archaeology: The Chillicothe Conference.* Kent: The Kent State University Press.

Bryan, L. 1991. *The Buffalo People: Prehistoric Archaeology on the Canadian Plains.* Edmonton: The University of Alberta Press.

Burenhult, G., ed. 1993. *The First Humans: Human Origins and History to 10,000 B.C.* The Illustrated History of Humankind, vol. 1. San Francisco: Harper San Francisco.

———. ed., 1994. *New World and Pacific Civilizations: Cultures of America, Asia and the Pacific.* The Illustrated History of Humankind, vol. 4. San Francisco: Harper San Francisco.

Campbell, T. N. 1958. "Origin of the Mescal Bean Cult." *American Anthropologist* 60: 156–160.

Cinq-Mars, J. 1979. "A Late Pleistocene Eastern Beringian Cave Deposit in the Northern Yukon," *Canadian Journal of Archaeology.* No. 3: 1–32.

———. 1990. "La Place des Grottes du Poisson-Bleu Dans La Prehistoire Beringienne," *Revista de Arqueologia Americana.* No. 1: 9–32.

Coe, M., Snow, D., and Benson, E. 1989. *Atlas of Ancient America.* New York: Facts on File.

Dancey, W. S. 1991. "A Middle Woodland Settlement in Central Ohio: A Preliminary Report on the Murphy Site (33LI212)." *Pennsylvania Archaeologist* vol. 61: 37–72.

———. 1992. "Village Origins in Central Ohio: The Results and Implications of Recent Middle and Late Woodland Research." In *Cultural Variability in Context: Woodland Settlements of the Mid-Ohio Valley*, ed. M. F. Seeman, pp. 24–29. Kent: The Kent State University Press.

"Dating an Ancient Russian 'Revolution.'" *Science News.* October 2, 1993.

Dillehay, T. 1987. "By the Banks of the Chinchihuapi," *Natural History*, 4/87: pp. 8–12.

Dixon, E. J. 1993. *Quest for the Origins of the First Americans.* Albuquerque: University of New Mexico Press.

Dobyns, H. F. 1966. Estimating Aboriginal American Population: An Appraisal of Techniques with a New Hemispheric Estimate. *Current Anthropology.* 7:395–444.

———. 1983. *Their Number Become Thinned.* Knoxville: The University of Tennessee Press.

Doyel, D. E., ed. 1992. *Anasazi Regional Organization and the Chaco System.* Anthropological Papers No. 5. Albuquerque: Maxwell Museum of Anthropology.

Duggins, D. O. 1983. "Marine Dominoes," *Equinox* 2: 43–57.

Eliade, M. 1964. *Shamanism: Archaic Techniques of Ecstasy.* Translated by W. R. Trask. New York: Bollingen Foundation.

———, ed. 1987. *The Encyclopedia of Religion.* New York: Macmillan.

Ellis, F. H., and Hammack, L. 1968. "The Inner Sanctum of Feather Cave, A Mogollon Sun and Earth Shrine Linking Mexico and the Southwest." *American Antiquity* 29: 25–44.

Erlandson, J. M. 1994. *Early Hunter-Gatherers of the California Coast.* New York and London: Plenum Press.

Estabrook, B. 1982. "Bone Age Man." *Equinox* 1: 84–96.

Fagan, B. M. 1991. *Ancient North America: The Archaeology of a Continent,* New York: Thames and Hudson, Inc.

Fisher, R. 1977. Missions to the Indians of British Columbia. In *Early Indian Village Churches: Wooden Frontier Architecture in British Columbia,* eds. J. Veillette and G. White, pp. 1–11. Vancouver: University of British Columbia Press.

Fladmark, K. R. 1979. "Routes: Alternate Migration Corridors for Early Man in North America." *American Antiquity* 44:55–69.

———. 1986. "Getting One's Berings." *Natural History* 11/86: 9–19.

Fowler, M. L. 1969. The Cahokia Site. *Explorations into Cahokia Archaeology.* Illinois Archaeological Survey, Inc. Bulletin No. 7. Urbana: University of Illinois.

———. 1974. *Cahokia: Ancient Capital of the Midwest.* Addison-Wesley Module in Anthropology No. 48. Menlo Park: Cummings.

———. 1975. "A Precolumbian Urban Center on the Mississippi." *Scientific American* 23: 92–101.

———. 1989. The Cahokia Atlas: A Historical Atlas of Cahokia Archaeology. Illinois Historic Preservation Agency Studies in Illinois Archaeology, No. 6. Springfield: Illinois Historic Preservation Agency.

Fraser, S. *Letters and Journals 1806–1808,* ed. W. Kaye Lamb. Toronto: Macmillan Co of Canada, 1960.

Friedman, R. 1995. "Return to Ozette." *Federal Archeology.* Winter/Spring 1995, pp. 16–19.

Frison, G. 1978. *Prehistoric Hunters of the High Plains.* New York: Academic Press.

Furst, P. T. 1972. *Flesh of the Gods: The Ritual Use of Hallucinogens.* New York: Praeger Publishers.

Gardner, J. L., ed. 1986. *Mysteries of the Ancient Americas: The New World Before Columbus.* Pleasantville, N.Y.: The Reader's Digest Association, Inc.

Gibbons, A. 1993. "Geneticists Trace the DNA Trail of the First Americans." *Science* 259: 312–313.

Greber, N. with Griffin, J. B. 1983. *Recent Excavations at the Edwin Harness Mound, Liberty Works, Ross County, Ohio.* Kent: Kent State University Press.

Greber, N. B., and Ruhl, K. G. 1989. *The Hopewell Site: A Contemporary Analysis Based on the Work of Charles C. Willoughby.* Boulder: Westview Press.

Grinnell, G. B. 1962. *Blackfoot Lodge Tales. The Story of a Prairie People.* Lincoln: University of Nebraska Press.

Gruhn, R. 1988. "Linguistic Evidence in Support of the Coastal Route of Earliest Entry into the New World." *Man* 23:77–100.

Hall, H. 1990. *The Kelp Forest.* San Luis Obispo: Blake Publishing.

Hall, R. L. 1979. In Search of the Ideology of the Adena-Hopewell Climax. In *Hopewell Archaeology: The Chillicothe Conference.* eds D. Brose and N. Greber, pp. 258–265. Kent: The Kent State University Press.

———. 1985. "Medicine Wheels, Sun Circles, and the Magic of World Center Shrines." *Plains Anthropologist* 30: 181–193.

———. 1989. "The Cultural Background of Mississippian Symbolism." In *The Southeastern Ceremonial Complex: Artifacts and Analysis, The Cottonlandia Conference,* ed. P. Galloway. 239–308. Lincoln: University of Nebraska Press.

———. 1991. "Cahokia Identity and Interaction Models of Cahokia Mississippian." In *Cahokia and the Hinterlands: Middle Mississippian Cultures of the Midwest,* eds. T. E. Emerson and R. B. Lewis. pp. 3–34. Urbana: University of Illinois Press.

Halverson, J. 1987. "Art for Art's Sake in the Paleolithic." *Current Anthropology* 28: 63–88.

Harington, C. R. 1983. "The Woolly Mammoth." *Neotoma.* National Museums of Canada, No. 17.

———. 1989. "Pleistocene Vertebrate Localities in the Yukon." In *Late Cenozoic History of the Interior Basins of Alaska and the Yukon,* eds. L. D. Carter, T. D. Hamilton, and J. P. Galloway. U.S. Geological Survey Circular 1026.

———. 1990. "The American Lion." *Neotoma.* National Museums of Canada, No. 27.

———. 1991. "North American Short-Faced Bears." *Neotoma.* National Museums of Canada. No. 29.

Hayden, B. 1990. "Nimrods, Piscators, Pluckers, and Planters: The Emergence of Food Production." *Journal of Anthropological Archaeology* 9: 31–69.

———. 1993. *Archaeology: The Science of Once and Future Things.* New York: W. H. Freeman & Co.

———, ed. 1992. *A Complex Culture of the British Columbia Plateau: Traditional Stl'átl'imx.* Vancouver: UBC Press.

———. 1993. "The Keatley Creek Site and Corporate Group Archaeology." *BC Studies,* Autumn 1993.

Hayden, B., and Cannon, A. 1982. "The Corporate Group as an Archaeological Unit." *Journal of Anthropological Archaeology* 1: 132–158.

Hayden, B., and Ryder, J. M. 1991. "Prehistoric Cultural Collapse in the Lillooet Area." *American Antiquity* 56: 50–65.

Heidenreich, C. 1971. *Huronia: A History and Geography of the Huron Indians 1600–1650.* Toronto: McClelland and Stewart Limited.

Hildebrandt, W. R., and Jones, T. L. 1992. "Evolution of Marine Mammal Hunting: A View from the California and Oregon Coasts." *Journal of Anthropological Archaeology* 11:360–401.

Hoffecker, J. F., Powers, W. R., and Goebel, T, 1993. "The Coloniza-tion of Beringia and the Peopling of the New World." *Science* 259: 46–53.

Holley, G. R., Dalan, R. A., and Smith, P. A. 1993. "Investigations in the Cahokia Site Grand Plaza." *American Antiquity* 58: 306–319.

Hopkins, D. M., ed. 1967. *The Bering Land Bridge*. Stanford: Stan-ford University Press.

Hopkins, D. M., Matthews, J. V., Schweger, C. E., and Young, S. B., eds. 1982. *Paleoecology of Beringia*. New York: Academic Press.

Hoyt, E. 1992. *Riding with the Dolphins: The Equinox Guide to Dol-phins and Porpoises*. Camden East, Ontario: Camden House.

Hungry Wolf, A. 1983. *Shadows of the Buffalo: A Family Odyssey Among the Indians*. New York: William Morrow and Company, Inc.

Hunter, A. F. 1902. "Notes on Sites of Huron Villages in the Town-ship of Medonte (Simcoe County)." *Annual Archaeological Report, Appendix to the Report of the Minister of Education, On-tario*, pp. 56–100.

Irving, W. N. 1987. "New Dates from Old Bones." *Natural History* 2/87: 8–13.

Irving, W. N., and C. R. Harington. 1973. "Upper Pleistocene Radiocarbon-Dated Artefacts from the Northern Yukon." *Sci-ence* 179: 335–340.

Jonaitis, A., ed. 1991. *Chiefly Feasts: The Enduring Kwakiutl Pot-latch*. Seattle and London: University of Washington Press.

Jones, T. L. 1991. "Marine Resource Value and the Priority of Coastal Settlement: A California Perspective." *American Antiq-uity* 56: 419–443.

Jones, T. L., ed. 1992. *Essays on the Prehistory of Maritime California*, Center for Archaeological Research at Davis Publications No. 10. Davis: University of California.

Judd, N. H. 1925. "Everyday Life in Pueblo Bonito." *National Geo-graphic*, September 1925.

Kehoe, T. F. 1987. "Corralling Life." *Wisconsin Academy Review*, March 1987, pp. 45–49.

Kirk, R., and Daugherty, R. D. 1978. *Exploring Washington Archaeology*. Seattle and Washington: University of Washing-ton Press.

Kirkland, F., and Newcombe, W. W. 1967. *The Rock Art of Texas In-dians*, Austin and London: University of Texas Press.

Knight, D. H. 1987. "Settlement Patterns at the Ball Site: A 17th Century Huron Village." *Archaeology of Eastern North America* 15: 177–188.

Knight, V. J. Jr. 1986. "The Institutional Organization of Mississippian Religion." *American Antiquity* 51: 675–687.

Koppel, T. 1992. "The Peopling of North America." *Canadian Geographic.* vol. 112, no. 5: pp. 54–65.

Kroeber, A. L. 1925. Handbook of the Indians of California. *Bureau of American Ethnology Bulletin 78.* Washington: Bureau of American Ethnology.

La Barre, W. 1964. *The Peyote Cult.* Hamden, Conn.: Shoe String Press.

Leechman, D. 1954. *The Vanta Kutchin.* Anthropological Series, no 33. Ottawa: Department of Northern Affairs and National Resources.

Lekson, S. H. 1987. "Great House Architecture of Chaco Canyon, New Mexico." *Archaeology* May/June 1987, 22–31.

Lekson, S. H., Windes, T. C., Stein, J. R., and Judge, W. J. 1988. "The Chaco Canyon Community." *Scientific American* 259: 100–109.

Lepper, B. T. 1988–1989. "An Historical Review of Archaeological Research at the Newark Earthworks." *Journal of the Steward Anthropological Society* Vol. 18: 118–140.

————. 1993. "The Newark Earthworks and the Geometric Enclosures of the Scioto Valley: Connections and Conjectures." Paper presented at *A View from the Core: A Conference Synthesizing Ohio Hopewell Archaeology,* 19–20 November 1993, Chillicothe, Ohio.

Lewis-Williams, J. D., and Dowson, T. A. 1990. "Through the Veil: San Rock Paintings and the Rock Face." *South African Archaeological Bulletin* 45: 5–16.

Lister, R. H., and Lister, F. C. 1981. *Chaco Canyon: Archaeology and Archaeologists.* Albuquerque: University of New Mexico Press.

Lubbock, Sir J. *Pre-historic Times: as Illustrated by Ancient Remains, and the Manners and Customs of Modern Savages.* London and Edinburgh: Williams and Norgate.

Lynott, M. J., and Monk, S. M. 1985. Mound City, Ohio, Archeological Investigations. *Midwest Archeological Center Occasional Studies in Anthropology,* no. 12. Lincoln: United States Department of the Interior.

Marshack, A. 1995. "Images of the Ice Age." *Archaeology* 48: 28–39.

McClintock, W. 1910. *The Old North Trail: Life, Legends and Religion of the Blackfeet Indians*. Reprint. Lincoln and London: University of Nebraska Press, 1968.

McGhee, R. 1989. *Ancient Canada*. Hull: Canadian Museum of Civilization.

Meighan, C. W. 1959. "The Little Harbor Site, Catalina Island: An Example of Ecological Interpretation in Archaeology." *American Antiquity* 24: 383–405.

Mellars, P. 1989. "Major Issues in the Emergence of Modern Humans." *Current Anthropology* 30: pp. 349–385.

Merrill, W. L. 1977. "An Investigation of Ethnographic and Archaeological Specimens of Mescalbeans (Sophora Secundiflora) in American Museums." *Museum of Anthropology, The University of Michigan Technical Reports*, no. 6. Ann Arbor: The University of Michigan.

Nabokov, P., and Easton, R. 1989. *Native American Architecture*. New York and Oxford: Oxford University Press.

Nelson, D. E., Morlan, R. E., Vogel, J. S., Southon, J. R., and Harington, C. R. 1986. "New Dates on Northern Yukon Artifacts: Holocene Not Upper Pleistocene," *Science* 232: 749–751.

Nikiforuk, A. 1991. *The Fourth Horseman: A Short History of Epidemics, Plagues, Famine and Other Scourges*. Toronto: Penguin Group.

Noble, D. G., ed. 1984. *New Light on Chaco Canyon*. Santa Fe: School of American Research Press.

Otten, C. F. 1986. *A Lycanthropy Reader: Werewolves in Western Culture*. Syracuse: Syracuse University Press.

Pacheco, P. 1988–1989. "Ohio Middle Woodland Settlement Variability in the Upper Licking River Drainage." *Journal of the Steward Anthropological Society* vol. 18, 87–117.

Pauketat, T. P. 1992. "The Reign and Ruin of the Lords of Cahokia: A Dialectic of Dominance." *Lords of the Southeast: Social Inequality and the Native Elites of Southeastern North America*, eds. Barker, A. W. and Pauketat, T. P. Archaeological Papers of the American Anthroplogical Association, no. 3.

———. 1994. *The Ascent of Chiefs: Cahokia and Mississippian Politics in Native North America*. Tuscaloosa: University of Alabama Press.

———, ed. 1993. *Temples for Cahokia Lords: Preston Holder's 1955–1956 Excavations of the Kunneman Mound*. Memoirs Museum of Anthropology, University of Michigan. No. 26. Ann Arbor: University of Michigan.

Pauketat, T. P., and Emerson, T. E. 1991. "The Ideology of Authority and the Power of the Pot." *American Anthropologist* 93: 919–940.

Pfeiffer, S. 1983. "Demographic Parameters of the Uxbridge Ossuary Population." *Ontario Archaeology* 40: 9–14.

———. 1986. "Morbidity and Mortality in the Uxbridge Ossuary." *Canadian Journal of Anthropology* 5: 23–32.

Pielou, E. C. 1991. *After the Ice Age: The Return of Life to Glaciated North America.* Chicago and London: University of Chicago Press.

Pisias, N. 1979. "Model for Paleoceanographic Reconstructions of the California Current During the Last 8000 Years," *Quaternary Research* 11: 373–386.

Prufer, O. H. 1964. "The Hopewell Culture," *Scientific American*, vol. 211: 90–102.

Raab, L. M. 1992. "An Optimal Foraging Analysis of Prehistoric Shellfish Collecting on San Clemente Island, California." *Journal of Ethnobiology* 1: 63–80.

———. 1994. "Reassessing the Age and Importance of Southern California Maritime Societies Among Archaic-Stage Cultural Adaptations." Paper read at *59th Annual Meeting of the Society for American Archaeology* at Anaheim, California.

Raab, L. M., Bradford, K., Porcasi, J. F., and Howard, W. J. "Return to Little Harbor, Santa Catalina Island, California: A Critique of the Maritime Paleotemperature Model." *American Antiquity,* in press.

Ramenofsky, A. F. 1987. *Vectors of Death: The Archaeology of European Contact,* Albuquerque: University of New Mexico Press.

Ramsden, P. G., 1978. "An Hypothesis Concerning the Effects of Early European Trader Among Some Ontario Iroquois." *Canadian Journal of Archaeology* 2: 101–106.

Reeves, B. O. K. 1983. "Six Millenniums of Buffalo Kills," *Scientific American*, October, 1983, pp. 120–135.

———. 1993. "Iniskim: A Sacred Nitsitapii Religious Tradition." In *Proceedings of the First Joint Meeting of the Archaeological Society of Alberta and the Montana Archeological Society,* ed B. O. K. Reeves and M. A. Kennedy, pp. 194–260. Calgary: The Archaeological Society of Alberta.

Ritchie, J. C., Cinq-Mars, J., and Cwynar, L. C. 1982. "L'environnement tardiglaciaire du Yukon septentrional, Canada," *Geographie physique et Quaternaire* 36: 241–250.

Ryder, J. M., and Church, M. 1986. "The Lillooet terraces of Fraser River: a palaeoenvironmental enquiry." *Canadian Journal of Earth Sciences,* vol. 23: 868–885.

Sale, K., and Kelly, K. 1995. "Interview with the Luddite." *Wired,* June 1995. pp. 166–169 and 211–216.

Salls, R. A., Raab, L. M., and Bradford, K. G. 1993. "A San Clemente Island Perspective on Coastal Residential Structures and the Emergence of Sedentism." *Journal of California and Great Basin Anthropology* 15: 176–194.

Schultes, R. E., and Hofmann, A. 1975. *The Botany and Chemistry of Hallucinogens.* Springfield: Charles C. Thomas.

Schultz, J. W. 1962. *Blackfeet and Buffalo: Memories of Life among the Indians.* Edited by Keith C. Seele. Norman and London: University of Oklahoma Press.

Shafer, H. J. 1986. *Ancient Texans: Rock Art and Lifeways along the Lower Pecos.* San Antonio: Texas Monthly Press.

———. 1988. "The Prehistoric Legacy of the Lower Pecos Region of Texas." *Bulletin of the Texas Archeological Society* 59: 23–52.

Shetrone, H. C. 1931. *The Mound-Builders,* New York: D. Appleton and Company.

Silverberg, R. 1968. *Mound Builders of Ancient America.* Greenwich, Connecticut: New York Graphic Society Ltd.

Sioui, G. E. 1992. *For an Amerindian Autohistory.* Montreal and Kingston: McGill-Queens University Press.

———. 1994. *Les Wendats: Une civilisation meconnue.* Sainte-Foy: Les Presses de l'Université Laval.

Smith, B. D. 1989. "Origins of Agriculture in Eastern North America." *Science* vol 246: 1566–1571.

———. 1991. "Harvest of Prehistory." *The Sciences,* May/June 1991: 30–35.

Smull, J., and Cox, T., eds. 1989. *A Step into the Past: Island Dwellers of Southern California.* Fullerton: California State University and the Museum of Anthropology.

Sofaer, A., and Sinclair, R. M. 1986. "A Solar Pueblo Symbol: An Interpretation of a Fajada Butte Petroglyph." A paper presented at the *Oxford II Conference on Archaeoastronomy,* January 1986, at Merida, Mexico.

———. 1989. "Solar and Lunar Orientations of the Major Architecture of the Chaco Culture of New Mexico." In *Colloquio Internazionale Archeologia e Astronomia,* ed. Gieorigia Bretschneider, Venice: Rivista di Archeologia.

Sofaer, A., Marshall, M. P., and Sinclair, R. M. 1989. "The Great North Road: A Cosmo of the Chaco Culture of New Mexico." In

World Archaeoastronomy, ed. A. F. Aveni. Cambridge: Cambridge University Press.

Sofaer, A., Zinser, V., and Sinclair, R. M. 1979. "A Unique Solar Marking Construct." *Science* vol. 206: 283–291.

Squier, E. G., and Davis, E. H. 1848. *Ancient Monuments of the Mississippi Valley, comprising the results of extensive original surveys and explorations by E. G. Squier and E. H. Davis.* Smithsonian Contributions to Knowledge. Washington: Johnson Reprint Corporation, 1948.

Stiebing, W. H. Jr. 1993. *Uncovering the Past: A History of Archaeology.* Buffalo: Prometheus Books.

Stryd, A. H., and Lawhead, S., eds. 1978. *Reports of the Lillooet Archaeological Project.* National Museum of Man Mercury Series no. 73. Ottawa: National Museums of Canada.

Sturtevant, W. C., ed. 1978–1995. *Handbook of North American Indians.* Washington: Smithsonian Institution.

Swanton, J. 1911. *Indian Tribes of the Lower Mississippi Valley.* In Bulletin of American Ethnology, Bulletin 43. Washington, Smithsonian Institution.

Teit, J. A. 1900. "The Thompson Indians of British Columbia." *Memoirs, American Museum of Natural History.* vol. 1. New York: American Museum of Natural History.

———. 1906. "The Lillooet Indians." *Memoirs, American Museum of Natural History,* vol. 2. New York: American Museum of Natural History.

Thomas, C. 1894. *Report on the Mound Explorations of the Bureau of Ethnology.* Reprint. Washington: Smithsonian Institution Press, 1985.

Thorne, A. G., and Wolpoff, M. H. 1992. "The Multiregional Evolution of Humans," *Scientific American* 266: 76–83.

Thwaites, R. G., ed. 1896–1901. *The Jesuit Relations and Allied Documents.* 73 vols. Cleveland: Burrows Brothers.

Tooker, E. 1964. *An Ethnography of the Huron Indians 1615–1649.* Bureau of American Ethnology Bulletin 190. Washington: United States Congress.

Trigger, B. G. 1969. *The Huron: Farmers of the North.* Holt, Rinehart and Winston, New York.

———. 1973. *The Children of Aataentsic: A History of the Huron People to 1660.* Montreal and Kingston: McGill-Queen's University Press.

————. 1989. *A History of Archaeological Thought*. Cambridge: Cambridge University Press.

Trinkhaus, E., and Shipman, P. 1993. *The Neanderthals: Changing the Image of Mankind*. New York: Alfred A. Knopf.

Turner, Christy G. II. 1993. "Cannibalism in Chaco Canyon: The Charnel Pit Excavated at Small House Ruin by Frank H. H. Roberts, Jr." *American Journal of Physical Anthropology* 91: 421–439.

Turpin, S. 1988. "Seminole Sink: Excavation of a Vertical Shaft Tomb, Val Verde County, Texas." *Plains Anthropologist* 33, Memoir 22.

————. 1990. "Speculations on the Age and Origin of the Pecos River Style, Southwest Texas." In *Proceedings of the International Rock Art Conference and 16th Annual Meeting of the American Rock Art Research Association*, ed. S. Turpin, pp. 99–122. Austin: National Park Service, American Rock Art Research Association and the University of Texas at Austin.

————. 1991. *Pecos River Rock Art: A Photographic Essay*. San Antonio: Sandy McPherson Publishing Company.

————. 1992. "More Sacred Holes in the Ritual Landscape of the Lower Pecos River Region." *Plains Anthropologist*, vol. 37: 275–278.

————., ed. 1994. *Shamanism and Rock Art in North America*. Special Publication 1, San Antonio: Rock Art Foundation, Inc.

Van Dyk, J. 1990. "Long Journey of the Pacific Salmon." *National Geographic*, July, 1990, pp. 3–37.

Verbicky-Todd, E. 1984. *Communal Buffalo Hunting Among the Plains Indians*. Archaeological Survey of Alberta Occasional Paper No. 24, Edmonton: Alberta Culture.

Wagner, H. R. 1966. *Spanish Voyages to the Northwest Coast of America in the Sixteenth Century*. Amsterdam: N. Israel.

Waldman, C. 1985. *Atlas of the North American Indian*. New York and London: Facts on File Publications.

Warrick, G. 1989. "Trends in Huron Family, Household and Community Size, A.D. 900–A.D. 1650." In *Households and Communities: Proceedings of the 21st Annual Chacmool Conference*, eds. S. MacEachern, D. J. W. Archer, and R. D. Garvin, pp. 277–286. Calgary: Chacmool.

————. 1990. A Population History of the Huron-Petun, A.D. 900–1650. Ph.D. dissertation, McGill University.

Wicklein, J. 1994. "Spirit Paths of the Anasazi." *Archaeology* 47: 36–42.

Wilbert, J. 1987. *Tobacco and Shamanism in South America*, New Haven and London, Yale University Press.

Wilcox, D. R. 1993. "The Evolution of the Chacoan Polity." In *The Chimney Rock Archaeological Symposium*, eds. J. M. Malville and G. Matlock. Fort Collins: Rocky Mountain Forest and Range Experiment Station.

Williamson, R. A. 1984. *Living the Sky: The Cosmos of the American Indian*. Boston: Houghton Mifflin.

Windes, T. C. 1987. *Investigations at the Pueblo Alto Complex, Chaco Canyon, New Mexico, 1975–79*. Publications in Archaeology 18F Chaco Canyon Studies. Santa Fe: National Park Service.

Witthoft, J. 1949. "Green Corn Ceremonialism in the Eastern Woodlands." *Occasional Contributions from the Museum of Anthropology of the University of Michigan*, No. 13. Ann Arbor: University of Michigan Press.

Index